THE ORIGINAL
Issue n° 19 — Summer 2023

PART 1

For this issue's cover, inimitable actress TILDA SWINTON
is photographed in Paris by Katerina Jebb.

PART 2

The Book of the Season is THE ODYSSEY, a singable story
of heroes and gods inhabiting the world's first archipelago.

Thermal infrared
mosaic from the
NASA spacecraft,
*Mars Odyssey.*

In the window seat with no seat neighbour, as per this photograph by ALEC SOTH, a solitary journey becomes an ideal reading situation. Alone between A and B, a good book takes the reader to C and D as well. Wrapped in a cloak of transport-based anonymity, that reader becomes more open to inhabiting someone else's story.

# Indefinite

Here's a word: hiatus. It means 'a pause or break in continuity in a sequence or activity'. Sometimes, to communicate a not-quite-absolute finality, it gets preceded by another word: indefinite. Books don't have hiatuses, they have endings. But magazines do.

Or do they? As with any book, a given issue of a magazine is always there, even if they stop printing new ones. It can be reread and shared and discovered by new people. It can be collected, sought out by those who missed it the first time around. It can gain new resonances, as time goes on.

To all our readers, thank you. I hope we made you happy. It was always a thrill to create it, and its spirit will live on.

With love,
Seb

THE HAPPY READER — Bookish Magazine — Issue n° 19
The Happy Reader is a collaboration between Penguin Books and Fantastic Man

EDITOR-IN-CHIEF Seb Emina ART DIRECTOR Matthew Young EDITORIAL DIRECTORS Jop van Bennekom, Gert Jonkers MANAGING EDITOR Maria Bedford PICTURE RESEARCH Samantha Johnson PRODUCTION Katy Banyard MARKETING Liz Parsons BRAND DIRECTOR Sam Voulters ACTING BRAND DIRECTOR Danielle Pender MARKETING DIRECTOR Ingrid Matts PUBLISHER Stefan McGrath CONTRIBUTORS Vladislav Davidzon, Rob Doyle, Eliot Haworth, Rebecca May Johnson, Nicholas Jubber, Daniel Levin Becker, Deborah Levy, Jeremy Lewis, Sabine Mirlesse, Justin E. H. Smith, Todd van Hulzen THANK YOU Magnus Åkesson, Timothy Han, Olga Kominek, Rebecca Lee, Lucca Lutzky, Jamie MacRae, Penny Martin, Caroline Pretty, Anna Wilson.

PENGUIN BOOKS  20 Vauxhall Bridge Road London SW1V 2SA  info@thehappyreader.com  www.thehappyreader.com

# Snippets

Booky news, literary events and
nourishing info, for now and all time.

## FRANKENSTUFF

Mary Shelley's famous monster is having a bit of a moment. A new album by rock group The National
is called *First Two Pages of Frankenstein* thanks to singer Matt Berninger's smart little trick for beating
writers' block. 'When I feel stuck, I'll often grab a book off the shelf just to get some words in my head,
and the first two pages of *Frankenstein* ended up triggering the song "Your Mind Is Not Your Friend",'
he says, the song being the LPs penultimate track, featuring Phoebe Bridgers. Elsewhere, a new
horror-comedy film, *Lisa Frankenstein*, transposes the book's premise to an American high school
setting: it's 1989 and a student is trying to turn a Victorian corpse into the man of her dreams.

## REST STOP

Monmouth Service Area,
a popular rest stop on the
Garden State Parkway
in New Jersey, has been
renamed Judy Blume Service
Area, in honour of the
beloved author best-known
for her novels for children
and young adults.

## SUFFOLK

The score for *Lisa Frankenstein* is by Isabella Summers, otherwise
known as half of British indie rock band Florence and the Machine.
Summers also created the soundtrack for Netflix's adaptation of
*Lady Chatterley's Lover*, the scandalous novel by D. H. Lawrence,
and made a composition to accompany the paintings of Cy Twombly
incorporating poems – by Rilke, Yeats, Homer – that inspired him at
different times. These literary endeavours have childhood roots:
Summers' parents owned Reed Books, the popular second-hand
bookshop in Aldeburgh, Suffolk. 'It was never not an inspiring
place,' she tells *The Happy Reader* over a smash burger at lunchtime.

## STELLAR

A poem is being sent to Europa, the fourth largest of Jupiter's
moons and home to some of the most potentially-life-friendly
conditions in the Solar System. The poem, composed by US
Poet Laureate Ada Limón, will be engraved onto an explora-
tory spacecraft, perhaps in case of contact with literate beings,
or perhaps because it's just nice to know it's out there.
In making the multibillion-mile odyssey it will join a small,
but significant, tradition of extra-terrestrial poetry that also
includes Maya Angelou's 'A Brave and Startling Truth',
stowed on Orion's test flight in 2014, and Thomas Bergin's
'For a Space Prober', etched into the panel of a research
satellite that has been orbiting the Earth since 1961.

## FARM

Ethan Hawke has directed a new
film based on the life of the
Southern Gothic writer Flannery
O'Connor. It's a family movie, in
a sense: Ethan's daughter, Maya,
best known as Robin Buckley in
*Stranger Things*, takes on the
mantle of portraying O'Connor
as she seeks out a publisher for
her sardonic and often grotesque
fictions while living on a farm in
Milledgeville, Georgia.

## BUMBLE

Please be prepared to stumble across a bookshop or website offering the service known as 'blind date with a book'. The customer buys a book without knowing what it is. They must decide which one based on the thematic words printed on its wrapping paper: 'Metafiction, propaganda, Faustian, death of fascism'. 'Psychohistory, civilisation, space opera, intellectual'. These examples are from the blind date shelves at Upper Street Bookshop, London.

## COVERS

Gladstone's Library, in the Welsh village of Hawarden, has twenty-six rooms available to sleep in for the night, it being the only residential library in the UK. It also has a bistro.

## HEADS-UP

The Greek island of Hydra has a reputation as a sort of Mediterranean nephew of the great literary cities. Henry Miller, Leonard Cohen and Charmian Clift are among those who were part of an ever-shifting cast of writers associated with the island since the 1930s or so. A hundred years on, Hydra is frequented by highly chic and cultured travellers, and there's still a good chance of running into a bestselling author there, perhaps at the beach or possibly buying Leonard Cohen's novel *Beautiful Losers* at bookstore-slash-art-installation the Hydra Book Club. Located, mostly, at Hydra's Historical Archives Museum, but with occasional cameos in the world at large, the Hydra Book Club was created by Josh Hickey, a literary curator who says it is 'more interested in the community represented by a bookstore than it is in making money from book sales'. Hickey also runs a telephone hotline, on which can be heard Nancy from LCD Soundsytem reading the work of Walt Whitman.

## MY BAG

Ethiopian-born supermodel Liya Kebede has launched a range of dedicated book bags. For a while now, Kebede has been running a book-focused Instagram account called @Liyabrairie, so it's intriguing to see her segue into a full-fledged line of products for readers. Essentially an adjustable matrix of leather straps available in colours including khaki, terracotta and *nuit*, the bags can accommodate anything from a single book to a mini-TBR-pile. Thus, passers-by can appreciate your reading choices even when you're not reading them.

## TRAVEL

Idea for an unusual sabbatical: Go to James Joyce Irish Pub in Istanbul, Turkey. From there travel to James Joyce Pub in Athens, Greece, Le James Joyce in Lyon, France, James Joyce Irish Pub & Restaurant in Baltimore, USA, and James & Joyce Pub in Phuket, Thailand. Visit all 100 or so pubs named after the Irish writer.

## TALENT SHOW

This year's Hemingway Look-Alike Contest, in which contestants vie with one another to more closely resemble Ernest Hemingway, takes place from 20–22 July at Sloppy Joe's Bar in the Key West area of southwest Florida.

## MATERIAL

What do poets wear? Do they have different clothes to non-poets? If so, why? *Poets in Vogue*, a free exhibition running until 10 September at The Poetry Library in London's South Bank Centre sets out to investigate. It does this not only by comparing old photographs with the relevant verse but by also recreating several female poets' clothes, from the red dress Anne Sexton wore at readings to the asymmetric kaftan worn by Audre Lorde after her mastectomy. Sylvia Plath's iconic tartan skirt is the one original garment on display, thanks to a loan from its current owner, the feminist bookshop The Second Shelf.

# TILDA SWINTON

'Cover girl? Me?!' says Tilda Swinton in the short film *Caprice*. It's about an ordinary woman who gets physically teleported into the inside of a magazine then mysteriously billed as its next cover star. Thirty-seven years later, we are excited to welcome her into our own pantheon of cover interviews, though, unlike her character in *Caprice*, she is quite accustomed to being a celebrity, completely used to the trappings of her unique, hypnotic screen presence. In this landmark conversation with the novelist Deborah Levy, Tilda looks into both the past and future, seeking out the contours of how encounters with the work of writers such as Virginia Woolf and Muriel Spark shaped her personality and worldview. How did books affect her projects with Derek Jarman? What's on her to-be-read pile now? Two cultural giants connect through the time-honoured method of literary exchange.

Interview by
DEBORAH LEVY

Portraits by
KATERINA JEBB

## LONDON CALLING AUSTRIA

It is a Saturday afternoon, and here Tilda Swinton is at last. At first we had hoped to meet in Paris, where she was rehearsing an extra-ordinary live performance. Titled *Embodying Pasolini*, it was a collab-oration with the French fashion historian Olivier Saillard. I saw this show on a freezing night in December. Paris was festive and magic-al, with silver lights threaded through the branches of trees and hot roasted chestnuts on sale outside the Metro. Tilda's schedule is fran-tically busy and our interview was postponed, but that was fine with me. I was happy to sit in the front row and witness her become a silent, poised, flesh-and-blood mannequin displaying over thirty cos-tumes designed by Danilo Donati for the films of the visionary Italian director Pier Paolo Pasolini, including *Oedipus Rex*, *The Decameron* and *Salò*.

Now, I am back in London. It is 2.15pm, time for our Zoom call. Dressed in emerald green, Tilda lights up the screen of my laptop. I first glimpsed her on a bigger screen in Derek Jarman's arthouse movie *The Last of England* (1987) when I was twenty-seven. In this film, Tilda whirls, gasps and sobs in a flimsy wedding dress on the pebbles of Dungeness beach, lit by a blazing orange sunset. Why is she sobbing? Her handsome husband has been executed. Newly wid-owed, she tears off her wedding dress and actually eats it. It seemed to me, sitting in the dark of the cinema all those years ago, that Tilda was invigoratingly uninhibited and free in the way she expressed and embodied Jarman's preoccupations. She was both auteur and actor, creating with him a distinctive mood and aesthetic. I have seen Tilda in many films over the decades since. In every one of them, whether mainstream or arthouse, she is both a very skilled actor and a poet of cinema.

Yes, she has a big presence, even on a laptop: her beauty, her thought-drifts, her energy and intelligence.

DEBORAH: Hello? Hello, Matilda. Tilda, hello.
 TILDA: You can call me Matilda. That's my proper name.

D: I know and I love that name. I feel, Tilda, that I grew up with you in art. When I first saw the films you made with Derek Jarman, *The Last of England*, *Caravaggio* and so on, they were such huge influences on me. And then your performance in Sally Potter's *Orlando* just blew my mind and it still does. It's a pleasure and an honour to be in conversation.

T: That's the loveliest thing I could hear because it is what I'd always hoped, which is that you can meet through it all and that's a beautiful thing. I also have to tell you that *Real Estate* is right at the top of my favourite books. Are you in Paris now?

D: No, I'm in London speaking to you from my apartment here. I'm looking out of the window right now. The sky is grey. It's gently, eternally, persistently raining. And you are in Austria?

T: I'm in Austria because I'm working. We're starting, we're preparing, I think that's the right word. It's sort of that phase in-between deep development and pre-production. We're getting ready to shoot something in Ireland in March. So I'm here doing that.

D: Well, I have to tell you that, for this conversation, my laptop is perched on a pile of books so that we can see each other at eye level.

T: I think that's very appropriate.

D: I've just noticed that one of these books is a biography of Diane Arbus by Patricia Bosworth, and then underneath it is *The Rolling Stone Illustrated History of Rock and Roll*.

T: Ah, quite right, that should be there.

D: Let's talk about *Orlando*. Do you mind if we jump in there?

T: Jump, jump, jump, jump.

D: And why don't we talk about writing and reading and performing and how they are in conversation with each other? Because it seems to me that a writer kind of directs the gaze of the reader. 'Look there and also look here, look under the table, look under the sea.' There's another word for this, I guess it's called storytelling, but I'd prefer not to use that word right at this moment. So one of the things that strikes me about your performance as Orlando is that I always believe your gaze, and am interested in your gaze. I believe how you look at someone or something. At the same time, the camera is gazing at you, the actor. And then you invented the strategy of breaking the fourth wall, because in *Orlando* you gaze directly back at us, the audience — long before that became a thing. I think that started with Derek, is that right?

T: Yes, *Caravaggio*. We were shooting *Caravaggio* and I was very much in a complete sort of leaping-out-the-window beginner's mind about it. I'd never been on a set of any kind before. I remember it was the first close-up that I'd been accorded. And I remember just on instinct saying, because I sort of felt... I won't say I felt awkward, but I felt a little confused about the scrutiny of the camera at that particular moment when I wasn't in conversation with anybody else. It felt strange not to be in conversation with the one person who was looking at me. Because normally one's in dialogue with someone who's looking at you and this time there was no human, but there was a camera with a human who I loved very much behind it.

D: Derek Jarman?

T: I asked Derek, I said, 'Can I look back?' And of course being Derek, he said, 'Yeah.' And it definitely, definitely started something. When I worked in the theatre, which is such a long time ago, the thing that stopped me working in the theatre above all the other things that might have stopped me working in the theatre — which is quite a list — is the last piece of theatre that I made, which was this play called *Man to Man*, by Manfred Karge, which we did at the Royal Court. It was a one-woman show. And so I was talking to the audience. It was like stand-up. And I love that so much. I love that back and forth. And I love the fact that that's where the energy went. I remember after that thinking, 'Well, I can never ever go back to the fourth wall again. I mean, I'm spoiled.'

D: When I was writing the living autobiographies I was trying to find the equivalent of that gaze. A tone, a voice, a presence that was intimate but formal at the same time. To create both distance and intimacy. It's very hard to do.

T: Well, it is. I was thinking this morning about *Real Estate* and why I would put it on my *Desert Island* shortlist. I was basically asking myself why I read. During Covid I stopped reading completely. So recently I've been asking myself — beginning on milk and little pieces of bread — 'What do you want to read, you little timid sort of tortoise who's just getting your head out again? What do you want to read?' So then the question is, 'Why do I want to meet people?' And it's funny you should invoke the word *storytelling* because I realise, and this is a slightly sort of shorthand thing to say, and maybe we'll unpick it and discover it's not true, but I feel I'm much less interested in story than I am in experience and in atmosphere. When someone is present, and Virginia Woolf is very present in *Orlando* for sure, but also in her essays, which I love the most — and also, in a way, in *Mrs Dalloway*, but that's a different story — I think that presence is a very

```
    ~¬__,
  ((o\\o\))
      \\
       \\        ldb
 ___.o"^^"_..___
 ~~~~~~~~
```

**1. DESERT ISLAND**

Tilda has never been a guest on BBC Radio's *Desert Island Discs*, but Deborah has. Her desert island music included 'Black Is the Color of My True Love's Hair' by Nina Simone, and 'Diamonds and Rust' by Joan Baez. Her desert island book was *The Archetypes of the Collective Unconscious* by Carl Jung. Her desert island luxury was a silk sheet.

complex construct, which is honest but formal. That formality is a really important, sort of, basket to have underneath. That openness of heart, life is light and shade, things can just twist. Just when you think it's all quite gloomy, something quite funny will happen. That atmosphere is what I'm really interested in. So many of my favourite writers do exactly this. They turn up as a person and I meet them. That's why it meant something to me, a lot to me, when you said that you felt you met me. That's exactly how I want to be felt. And that's what I feel about writers who go into this particular territory. I think it's incredibly generous.

D: As Oscar Wilde may or may not have said: 'Be yourself; everyone else is already taken.'
 T: I've never heard that before. That's perfect.

D: I've just watched *Orlando* for the fifth time. It actually made me cry. I don't know why. It's that scene when one of Orlando's lovers, Shelmerdine, played by Billy Zane, has galloped off into the future.
 T: He's gone for good.

D: And it begins to rain. Sally Potter gives screen time to that mood, to all the consequences of courage as Orlando stares out at us in the rain. We know that Orlando, now embodied as a she, is going to lose everything because women of her era had no rights to property. She's going to lose her house.
 T: And the topiary has been turned into a teacup behind her! I read *Orlando* when I was, I would say about fifteen. And I feel that I have to declare at the border right now, before we go any further, Deborah, that I have a sort of guilty secret, which is that my entire life from whatever, five to twenty-one, I was a writer. I even went to Cambridge as a writer. I got my place as a writer, and I then stopped. So I had...

D: You read Literature at Cambridge?
 T: I was a poet and I got an exhibition as a poet. And then I stopped writing, and then I changed to Social and Political Science. And I was stymied. But when I read *Orlando*, I was a writer then. I mean, I was a poet all through my childhood years and absolutely clear that that was my life. Even to the sort of ridiculous extent of allowing the school to put my poems into national competitions and winning prizes. I mean there was a sort of capital P somehow on me. And so when I first read *Orlando*, I read it as the poet that Orlando is. It was about a posh boy — which I also felt I was at fourteen — who was very lonely and was an artist, and specifically a poet, and who

2. TOPIARY
—
The character of Orlando is based on Vita Sackville-West, Virginia Woolf's lover and a celebrated garden designer.

'I dream of succulents, the flow of carbon, and acid metabolism,' said Tilda, playing a sentient robot in 1987's *Friendship's Death*.

3. BIOGRAPHER
—
Virginia Woolf's father,
Leslie Stephen, was an
esteemed biographer.
He was also an accom-
plished mountaineer, the
first to reach the top
of Alphubel, Wildstrubel
and seven other peaks
in the Alps.

was looking for his tribe. And so for me, *Orlando* was a precarious autobiography. And then of course, later, when I read more Virginia Woolf and knew more about *Orlando*, I realised that it is very much a book about writing and reading. And that Virginia Woolf, of course, was the daughter of a <u>biographer</u> and had access to a big library. So that whole idea of *Orlando* being a biography is also really important. It's also got that magic formality. So yes, I mean, it was my absolute. I think I probably went to bed at school with it under my pillow, like so many of us. And then years later, Sally Potter in I think something like 1988 took me out to tea and put the book down on the table in front of me. I mean, that's all she did. And I was so... She said to me later, years later, she said, 'Had you read the book?' And I think I must have been so blindsided that I just couldn't speak. But it was an absolute dream come true. Not only because it was that book, but also because it was her and because it was this film that we made, which is so... It gave me the possibility to... I always think that becoming a performer has been my way of writing all these years. On one hand you could say it's my way of avoiding writing on paper, but it's definitely been my way of writing. And I'm kind of always joking, saying, 'If I just stop making films, I would then get down to doing the writing I want to do.' But it is a way of writing. And this film that she wanted to make and the way she wanted to make it very much gave me the capacity to sort of rise to that or sync to it.

D: It could have been made yesterday.

T: Can you believe it's thirty years old? It's so fresh, isn't it?

D: A major work of art.

T: Sally was writing it painstakingly, and during that development period, preparation, whatever you call it, I would go to where she lived pretty much every day and sit with her and read what she'd written. And we would talk about every single beat. And it was such a privilege and such an enjoyable process. I mean, it did eventually take us five years, which now in my life is nothing. I mean, I've worked on films that have taken so much longer that that's really a lick and a spit. But it felt at that stage...

D: Sally Potter's script is so very skilled. Pitch perfect. I love the scene headings: 'Death', 'Politics', 'Poetry', 'Sex', 'Love', etcetera. Well, those are things we want to encounter in a book. So I guess you're saying, 'Well, I am Orlando,' in the way that Pasolini, when he was making *Oedipus Rex*, said, 'I am Oedipus Rex. I am the child in the prologue.'

T: Yeah, yeah, yeah. And I think that's definitely why it was able for me to feel so, what I call varnishless, which is what I love the most. I mean, I'm really, really not interested in acting at all. And I'm certainly not interested in performative performance. And so this was a real, in a way, it was a sort of template. I mean, it was the first film that I'd been in every frame of. When you're in every frame of a film, it's a particular privilege and a particular responsibility but the joy of it, the grace of it is that you can guide the mood like a writer can. You are guiding the atmosphere and the mood. And especially with this device of looking to the camera, it was about company. It was about you and me, we're together in this, babe, and we're going on this journey.

D: So when you read Literature at university, was Woolf on the syllabus? I mean, who was on your reading list?
    T: No, I don't think she was.

D: That doesn't surprise me at all.
    T: I did a very strange degree because I did Social and Political Science, which is a Part Two at Cambridge but I did it as a Part One. And then I switched because by then I had made lots of friends who were interested in the theatre and they were doing plays. They were either playwrights or directors or performers. And they asked me to come and do plays with them. And I directed one. And then after that, I was just in them. And I just spent so much time doing plays that I didn't have time to do anything else. So I switched to a Literature Part Two. I missed out on all the Anglo-Saxon stuff, which I'm actually slightly sad about. I think I would've rather loved that. I was very fixated in the moments of my dissertation on Hardy's women. I was very into Hardy for some reason. And what else? Milton.

D: Do you still write poetry?
    T: I very, very occasionally write poetry only for myself and I write essays. I've written essays for a while actually. I really like writing essays. And it all started, again as everything does, Deborah, with Derek. Because years and years and years later, after darling Derek had left the building, I was in... I mean he went in '94, and so many people did in that moment. I always say it's like a trapdoor, everybody just sort of vanished somehow. And my way of vanishing was to have twins and go and live in the Highlands, which I'm very happy that I did. But I completely sort of lost touch with everything London-based. And I wasn't really working. I was looking after my twins on a farm, and then I was asked in... Oh my God, I need to know the dates of things. Well, I can work out when it was. But basically it was about ten years later and I was asked by the Edinburgh

Tilda is photographed
in Paris in the home of
Katerina Jebb, her long-
time friend. Indeed, they
used to share this house
and it was known as 'The
Commune'. The coat is
by Chanel.

Film Festival to deliver their inaugural Edinburgh Festival speech. And they called it the Derek Jarman speech. I said immediately, 'No.' And the internal subtitle was, 'Because I can't write.' And then I just decided to do it. And that was the start. And I really enjoyed, not only funnily enough writing these essays, but occasionally delivering them. I'm very interested in that. In fact, I saw a beautiful thing that you did the other day. I was puttering around and I found a lovely thing of you, I can't remember which festival it was. Was it Folkestone? Of you delivering or reading a beautiful thing you wrote about being at Prospect Cottage?

D: Yes. Your presence was very much there when I stayed at Prospect Cottage. I actually watched you read that <u>letter</u> to Derek on YouTube. It's such a beautiful letter. Tough talking. You delivered it quite fast. I like your pace. Whenever anything starts with 'Dear someone', there tends to be a rather slow pace. Maybe slower than the thoughts that make up the letter.

T: Well, I was writing to him and that was, in a way, the nature of our conversation. If you know him, you know there were no flies on him.

D: I noticed when I stayed at Prospect Cottage that there were a lot of books by Gaston Bachelard in Derek's bookcase.

T: Yes. Yes.

D: *The Poetics of Space, The Poetics of Reverie.*

T: Absolutely, always. Oh, James Hillman, too. Derek was always giving me copies of James Hillman. Do you know James Hillman?

D: Yes.

T: I don't know why. I found them the other day. At Prospect Cottage they've got about five different James Hillman books inscribed in brown by Derek. He definitely wanted me to read them. And, of course, a lot of William Blake. We actually used to read William Blake to each other. And what else? Wilfred Owen. Again, this is about the work that we would make. I always say this to people — you'll understand this when I say that the life was the thing, and I always think the life was the trunk and the films were just leaves. They weren't even branches. The branch was our interest in Wilfred Owen. And then he was, 'Let's make a film, the *War Requiem*.' And then off it goes. But the trunk was still there and even the branch was still there. So we were reading Wilfred Owen to each other long before we had the idea of making *War Requiem*. And will you remind me, I know that you met him in, was it the Everyman?

4. LETTER
—
'This is what I miss, now that there are no more Derek Jarman films: the mess, the cant, the poetry, Simon Fisher Turner's music, the real faces, the intellectualism, the bad-temperedness, the good-temperedness, the cheek, the standards, the anarchy, the romanticism, the classicism, the optimism, the activism, the glee, the bumptiousness, the resistance, the wit, the fight, the colours, the grace, the passion, the beauty.' (Last sentence of Tilda's letter to Derek Jarman, delivered as a speech at the Edinburgh Film Festival in 2002.)

D: No, no, it was the Gate Cinema, Notting Hill Gate. I was eighteen. It was my gap year before university. I walked past the Gate Cinema a few times and peered in. I liked what the people working there were wearing. It's a very shallow story, Tilda.

T: No, no, no. It's very important.

D: I just thought they looked cool and that they looked like my sort of people.

T: You were looking for your tribe.

D: I was. I was. And I thought, 'Oh, well, maybe.' And then, boom! There was an advert in the *Evening Standard* for staff at the Gate Cinema! I remember thinking very carefully about what to wear at the interview and wondering whether I would be cool enough. And my mother screaming at me as I left the house because I was wearing big gold wedge platforms. 'You'll never get a job dressed like that.' Our poor, confused mothers, beloved mothers.

T: Oh my God.

D: And so in 1979, I think, the Gate was screening *Jubilee*. And Derek used to come into the cinema. As you know, he was just so friendly, cultured and charismatic and he didn't feel above talking to the eighteen-year-old bookish young woman in gold platforms making the popcorn... Anyway, you went to boarding schools?

T: Yeah.

D: So was reading a big part of your school life?

T: It was and it wasn't. I mean, I used to read about groups and... One of my great favourites was *Jennings*. Did you ever read the *Jennings* books? By Anthony Buckeridge?

Deborah: No.

T: I think I must have taken them from my brother's shelves. It's about a schoolboy and all his mates and all the japes and scrapes they get into and the terrible masters. The one bad teacher was Mr Watson, I think. The nice teacher was Mr Carter. And it was about fellowship and companionship. There is a whole string of them, probably about twelve. And I binged. I read every single one of them religiously. I'm talking about age eleven, twelve, thirteen. I mean, was Jane Austen as amusing as *Jennings*? Sometimes, but usually not. Partly, by the way, because those girls, I couldn't understand why they were so interested in the things they were interested in. But *Jennings*, I got it. I really was interested in trying to get to the top of the tree to see what was in that nest. But I wasn't so interested in machinations about finding a husband.

D: The boys in the *Jennings* books aren't looking for a wife.

T: No. They're looking for nests with interesting things in them and adventures and skulduggery. I have to say Robert Louis Stevenson was always there for the same reason. *Robinson Crusoe* and *Treasure Island* and all of that.

D: Adventures.

T: Adventure stories. Yeah. And Nancy Mitford! I think because of the fellowship, again, the group, the jollity. When you are sent away to boarding school when you're ten, what are the vitamins you lack? You lack that home. I mean, Nancy Mitford books are almost all about a family. And even when they're not, they're about that family feeling and I love that. I looked for that.

D: What about the *Just William* books?

T: Oh, I love *Just William*. I still love *Just William*. In fact, my children's father and I adore *Just William* and read *Just William* to my children. My son adores *Just William*. What else now? Hang on. Gosh. What did I read at school?

D: There are so many books in one's life. I think the ones that surface are interesting. Who were you reading when you were writing poetry?

T: I had a real passion, a sort of real crush on Dylan Thomas for a long time. And then a darker but more intense crush on Sylvia Plath. But complicated. And John Donne, I was completely crazy about John Donne for years. I remember actually having a very spiky argument with somebody who was saying that Donne was just nothing compared to Shakespeare. And I went head-to-head, a sort of silly thing to do, but I was prepared to go to the end for Donne.

D: How do you feel now reading *Ariel*? The big, deep, dark Plath poems? I read them in my twenties and I've read them every decade since.

T: I haven't looked at them for a long time and I think there's a reason for that. I think I've been slightly, what we call in Scotland 'hanging off'. I mean, like you, I love reading things every five years. I'll read *Orlando* every five years. It's like a health check. And it always is a different book, by the way. I read *Great Expectations* about every five years. But I'm due a reread of Sylvia Plath, so I'll let you know how it strikes me. How does it strike you now?

'*Orlando* was my absolute.
I think I probably went to
bed at school with it under
my pillow.'

# Total Tilda

A comprehensive list of movie appearances. With the exception of TV roles, short films, theatre, poetry, audiobook narration and other kinds of project, this is Tilda's full resumé.

*Asteroid City* (2023)
Elizabeth

*Problemista* (2023)
Elizabeth

*Guillermo del Toro's Pinocchio* (2022)
Wood Sprite /
Death (voice)

*The Eternal Daughter* (2022)
Julie Hart /
Rosalind Hart

*Three Thousand Years of Longing* (2022) ↓
Alithea

*Memoria* (2021)
Jessica Holland

*The French Dispatch* (2021) ↑
J.K.L. Berensen

*The Souvenir Part II* (2021)
Rosalind

*Last and First Men* (2020)
Narrator (voice)

*The Personal → History of David Copperfield* (2019)
Betsey Trotwood

*Uncut Gems* (2019)
Anne 'Adley's Auction Manager' (voice)

*The Dead Don't Die* (2019)
Zelda Winston

*Avengers: Endgame* (2019)
The Ancient One

*The Souvenir* (2019)
Rosalind

*Suspiria* (2018)
Dr Klemperer /
Madame Blanc /
Helena Markos (as Lutz Ebersdorf)

*Isle of Dogs* (2018)
Oracle (voice)

*War Machine* (2017)
German Politician

*Okja* (2017)
Lucy / Nancy
Mirando

*Doctor Strange* (2016)
The Ancient One

*Letters from Baghdad* (2016)
Gertrude Bell
(voice)

*The Seasons in Quincy: Four Portraits of John Berger* (2016)
Self

*Hail, Caesar!* (2016)
Thora Thacker /
Thessaly Thacker

*A Bigger Splash* (2015)
Marianne Lane,
Performer

*Trainwreck* (2015)
Dianna

*Listen to Me Marlon* (2015)
Performer

*The Grand Budapest Hotel* (2014)
Madame D.

*The Zero Theorem* (2013)
Dr Shrink-Rom

*Snowpiercer* (2013)
Mason

*Only Lovers Left Alive* (2013)
Eve

*Moonrise Kingdom* (2012)
Social Services

*We Need to Talk ↓ About Kevin* (2011)
Eva Khatchadourian

*The Chronicles of Narnia: The Voyage of the Dawn Treader* (2010)
White Witch

*I Am Love* (2009)
Emma Recchi ↗

*The Limits of Control* (2009)
Blonde

*The Curious Case of Benjamin Button* (2008)
Elizabeth Abbott

*Burn After Reading* (2008)
Katie Cox

*The New Ten Commandments* (2008)
Self

*The Chronicles of Narnia: Prince Caspian* (2008)
White Witch

*Julia* (2008)
Julia

*Derek* (2008)
Narrator
(voice)

*Michael Clayton* (2007)
Karen Crowder

*The Man from London* (2007)
Camélia

*Faceless* (2007)
Narrator

*Strange Culture* (2007)
Hope Kurtz

*Stephanie Daley* (2006)
Lydie Crane

*The Chronicles of Narnia: The Lion, the Witch and the Wardrobe* (2005)
White Witch ↙

*Broken Flowers* (2005)
Penny

*Constantine* (2005)
Gabriel

*Thumbsucker* (2005)
Audrey Cobb

*The Statement* (2003)
Annemarie Livi

*Young Adam* (2003)
Ella Gault

*Adaptation.* (2002)
Valerie Thomas

*Teknolust* (2002)
Rosetta / Ruby /
Marinne / Olive

*Vanilla Sky* (2001)
Rebecca Dearborn

*The Deep End* (2001)
Margaret Hall

*Possible Worlds* (2000)
Joyce

*The Beach* (2000)
Sal

*The Protagonists* (1999)
Actress

*The War Zone* (1999)
Mum

*Love Is the Devil: Study for a Portrait of Francis Bacon* (1998)
Muriel Belcher

*Conceiving Ada* (1997)
Ada Byron King

*Female Perversions* (1996)
Eve Stephens

*Remembrance of Things Fast: True Stories Visual Lies* (1994)
Actress

*Blue* (1993)
Narrator (voice)

*Wittgenstein* (1993)
Lady Ottoline
Morrell

*Orlando* (1992)
Orlando ↗

*Man to Man* (1992)
Ella / Max Gerike

*Edward II* (1991) →
Isabella

*The Party: Nature Morte* (1991)
Queenie

*The Garden* (1990)
Madonna

*Melancholia* (1989)
Musician

*Play Me Something* (1989)
Hairdresser

*War Requiem* (1989)
The Nurse

*Das andere Ende der Welt* (1988)
Actress

*The Last of England* (1987)
The Maid

*Friendship's Death* (1987)
Friendship

*Aria* (1987)
Young Girl

*Caprice* (1986)
← Lucky

*Egomania: Island Without Hope* (1986)
Sally

*Caravaggio* (1986)
Lena

D: It's hard to figure out how Plath might have talked about those poems had she lived. I'm so admiring and aghast by the writing in *Ariel*. A poem of Plath's called 'The Couriers', brought up something very interesting for me. When I was studying theatre at Dartington College of Arts, I had to play Masha in Chekhov's play *Three Sisters*. And I was very reluctant to do so. I didn't want to act. And I suppose the director thought that the sulky young woman with high cheekbones resembled Masha's moodiness. A terrible mistake. Anyway, *Three Sisters* starts with Masha reading a poem by Pushkin out loud:

> *A green oak by the circling sea.*
> *An oak with a chain of gold...*
> *An oak with a chain of gold...*

So there I am, all of nineteen. I haven't read Pushkin and I can't work out why Masha is mournfully reading this poem or what it means. And the director doesn't seem to be able to explain either. Then I reread Sylvia Plath a few years ago and she's written a poem about her wedding ring in 'The Couriers':

> *A ring of gold with the sun in it?*
> *Lies. Lies and a grief.*

And I thought, 'Oh, that's Masha. She is the green oak by the circling sea. An oak circled with a chain of gold.' I really love the way that reading throws light on other books.

T: Yes, the ways books talk to each other. I was thinking of the books that I brought to Austria, which of course I'm not really able to read because I'm working. I'll go and get them. I'll get you my pile. Hang on. They're just here. I'm always reading about seven things at once. [*She gets up and returns with a pile of books.*] So these are, I think, all of them, carefully curated, because I like to read them all at once. [*Tilda starts holding them up to the screen so that Deborah can read the titles.*]

D: *On Tyranny: Twenty Lessons from the Twentieth Century* by Timothy Snyder.

T: Have you read it?

D: No.

T: He's an historian, an American historian with expertise in Russia and specifically Ukraine. His other, longer book, which is amazing, is called *The Road to Unfreedom*. It explains, well, not exactly, I don't know, but gets as close as I can imagine anybody getting to explain why Ukraine and Russia are in this bind right now. It's completely fascinating. Then this of course.

D: *Flights* by Olga Tokarczuk. Yes, that's wonderful, isn't it?

T: I love it. It's actually very worn. And then this, I've only just started. I've been wanting to read this for ages.

D: *In Memory of Memory* by Maria Stepanova. Yes. That's really interesting. 'Too much past' is what Stepanova says. 'Too much past.' It's my favourite line.

T: I started this.

D: *The Crane Wife* by CJ Hauser. Why *The Crane Wife*?

T: I'll tell you why. Because it's a memoir in essays. I read some very glowing reviews. But I'm particularly interested, and I'll be honest, as someone who's been writing essays for a while, I'm trying to find a way... Well, I'm actually in the process of trying to put together a book of my essays. So Michel de Montaigne's next door as well. [*She holds up another book.*] Have you read this?

D: *Miss Aluminum* by Susanna Moore. No, I haven't read it yet.

T: Susanna Moore's memoir, which, again, I've only just started. And this. I haven't started at all, but he writes really well, Rupert Everett. I think I just got it because it's the latest... about him making his <u>film of Oscar Wilde</u>, which I really liked, by the way. I thought it was really, really well done.

D: Tilda, would you hold up the Rupert Everett again so I can see the title? [*Tilda holds up the book.*] *To the End of the World – Travels with Oscar Wilde.*

T: There we go. But talking about books talking to each other, when I read five or six books together like that, I mean, sometimes I've got time to read one at a time, and then I just go in and don't do anything, just eat. But when I'm working and preoccupied, I'll take a chapter from that and a chapter from that and a chapter from that. And if I've curated them well enough, they do talk to each other.

D: I guess a writer is only as interesting as how they think. For myself, if I don't enjoy how a writer thinks, I stop reading.

T: What are your reading, not habits, but what is your reading story at the moment? I mean, do you read when you write?

D: Oh no. And like you, I found it very difficult to read during the pandemic, during the lockdowns.

T: Strange, wasn't it?

D: It was so strange. I watched films, mostly. When I write, I can't

5. FILM OF
OSCAR WILDE
—
*The Happy Prince* (2018),
Everett's poignant
directorial debut, tracing
the writer's last days
before he died, famously,
in L'Hôtel in Paris, which
is still open and boasting
an 'Oscar Wilde Suite',
though the actual room
in which he stayed was
at some point turned into
the bar area.

read at all. I often listen to music just to find a mood, something that has no words. As for my reading at the moment, it is everything by Sigrid Nunez. Have you read her?

T: Which one are you reading?

D: Okay, so I started off with *The Friend*, which I thought was pretty extraordinary. Have you read it?

T: I have indeed.

D: Then I read *What Are You Going Through*. The title is a quote from the philosopher Simone Weil. [*Deborah gets up to shut a window. Rain is falling onto her sofa.*] Weil thought that was the only important question to ask anyone at the time she was living and writing. [*Deborah sits down again. Tilda looks very poised on her chair in Austria.*] But my favourite Nunez book is an early one called *Mitz*. It's all about Leonard Woolf's pet marmoset.

T: Oh.

D: And you would love it.

T: [*looking at her phone*] I see it. Now I'm ordering it. I don't normally do this. How fabulous. I've seen pictures of that marmoset. I'm writing it down now. *Mitz*.

D: So Leonard Woolf adopts a marmoset that belongs to the Rothschilds. He likes to take in sickly things and extraordinary things. And Nunez uses Leonard Woolf's own autobiographies and various letters and the diaries of Virginia Woolf to construct this whole story about Mitz the marmoset.

Mitz was captured in the South American jungle. And when Vita Sackville-West comes to the Woolfs' house, someone has sent Virginia a panel of impaled butterflies from South America. They're hanging on the wall and Vita holds up Mitz so that it can see the butterflies. 'Do you recognise any of them? Are any of them your friends?' Vita asks. Mitz loved pearls. Vita had taught Virginia how to recognise a fake pearl. And so Virginia was always interested in the way that Mitz played with her pearls and the pearls of guests. Those are the three Nunez books I've read so far.

T: How fabulous. Shall I tell you a secret if you promise not to write it?

D: Okay.

T: So a complete secret?

D: Yes.

[*Tilda proceeds to tell the secret. Time passes. Rain continues to falls gently on London. Tilda leans into the screen from Austria. Her voice is precise, succinct, her eyes are clear and bright. Her pale skin is flawless and otherworldly. Deborah takes a few sips of coffee. After a while they change the subject.*]

D: I'm also a big fan of Muriel Spark.
  T: Muriel Spark. She's absolutely my North Star.

D: *The Prime of Miss Jean Brodie* is my favorite Spark. And I actually think that you should play Miss Jean Brodie. I mean, I think you have to do that.
  T: I looked at the film and the thing is, Deborah, the film's kind of great.

D: It's perfect.
  T: It's perfect.

D: Maggie Smith is perfect as Miss Jean Brodie.
  T: Perfect.

D: I admire the way Spark encourages us to fall in love with a fascist. That is very skilled writing. What other writer could do that?
  T: Nobody else.

D: She manages to get us onside with the crazier parts of Jean Brodie.
  T: Totally. You're in love with her.

D: I really want things to work out for Jean Brodie because she's the only progressive-seeming person in the book, apart from the art teacher.
  T: Muriel Spark really understood the glamour of fascism. And she's also looking at what it is to be a twelve-, thirteen-year-old girl. And we're very, very much looking for that. We're looking for glamour and we're looking for someone who gives us that sense of fellowship.

D: Even though the Maggie Smith film is perfect, I would like to adapt *The Prime of Miss Jean Brodie* for film. Because, as you know, the world is suffering from tyrants and terrible governance at the moment.
  T: You have to read this. [*She holds up the Timothy Snyder book again.*] You have to go read it now.

D: I'm going to order it right away. [*Deborah picks up her phone and orders* On Tyranny *right away.*]

   T: As the beginning of the predevelopment of our Jean Brodie project, I want to read you this thing that I read this morning.

D: Yes, please.

   T: So Timothy Snyder's book is constructed as a series of twenty lessons from the twentieth century about how to avoid or how to notice, how to recognise fascism. The first one is 'Do not obey in advance,' which is so brilliant. He writes, 'Most of the power of authoritarianism is freely given. In times like these, individuals think ahead about what a more repressive government will want, and then offer themselves without being asked. A citizen who adapts in this way is teaching power what it can do.'
   Anyway, I won't read more, but it's so brilliant.

D: That's the beginning of the Jean Brodie project, isn't it?
   T: That's right. That's the beginning.

D: Do you have a title yet for the book of essays you're writing?
   T: Do you know, I actually do. I have a publisher. The lovely Rizzoli are going to publish it. But I'm a bit shy about giving the title…

D: Oh, you don't have to.
   T: Here's the thing, and you will maybe sympathise. Possibly not, no. I think my sense is that you've never felt this, sort of, cauterised, but I have a selection of essays and they are mostly letters to people. To start, David Bowie and, in fact, Pedro Almodóvar, and my son and Derek and various other people, but also about cinema and culture in general. And I have most of them. But my beautiful publisher says, 'You need one more.' Because the last one was from a couple of years ago, so I'm stuck. I'm going to write it soon and then it's going to be done and I can think about other things.

D: Does it have to be a letter? They're all letters, so you have to write one more?
   T: No, it doesn't have to be a letter. I think it's going to be an essay of some kind. I don't know what it was like with your first book, because this is my first book. Funnily enough, do you know what? Bringing it round to our favourite theme, what it reminds me of — and thinking of this makes me feel better about all of this — is when we made *The Last of England* and *The Garden*. Because *The Last of England*, which was the first film we made in that way, was sort of a series

6. DAVID BOWIE
—

There was a Tumblr blog called TildaStardust dedicated to the theory that Tilda and Bowie were in fact the same person. That theory was disproved in 2013 when Tilda starred as Bowie's wife in the video for his single 'The Stars (Are Out Tonight)'.

ASCII lightning adapted from an original by Evan M Corcoran (emc) of home movies of us just travelling around the world and us just puttering around with some stones and a candle and whatever else. And then at a certain point, we put them all out in front of us, like an anthology of poetry. And we went, 'Well, there's that one.' And then we moved it around and we said, 'We need something between this and that, so let's go away and shoot a boy with a flare in the water.' And we went away and did it. So that's what I have to do. I have to go away and find the boy with the flare in the water and then it's all going to be done. And then I will have written a book.

D: But isn't the boy with the flare in the water, going back to *Orlando*, the poet in you? So you could write about those early days of writing poetry.

T: I think you are absolutely right. I hadn't thought of that... To go to the beginning rather than... Because I suppose I'm feeling as if I have to round something up or even bring something up to date. And frankly these days, and this is a longer conversation, I feel so... It's not that I feel unsure of the present. It's partly to do with age, but I feel so interested in the beginnings and the roots. I can't really look at now. I can't really see it. I can see clearly, more clearly, the roots. So I think that's great.

D: I hope we meet in Paris.

T: Let's meet in Paris. When are you next there?

D: Soon.

T: Oh, good. And we're going to talk about everything.

D: I can't wait. Bye, Tilda.

T: Bye, Deborah.

When Tilda exits the screen, the room feels empty. Tilda's big presence is like stardust falling through a grey sky. I put away the books that have been propping up my laptop. The day after this conversation, Tilda texts me with a list of writers who did not make it into the interview.

These are some of the people whom I keep close.
I probably found most of them in my teenage years.
George Eliot
Elizabeth Taylor
Evelyn Waugh

Tilda was sitting below a portrait of Marcel Duchamp by German-French photographer Gisèle Freund.

Margaret Drabble

Graham Greene

John Berger

PG Wodehouse

Hafiz

James Salter (later, probably as a student)

Chinua Achebe

Tolstoy. *War and Peace* blew my mind. I was so grateful not
to have read it earlier,

when I might have missed out the war bits.

Chekhov's short stories

Walter Benjamin

Gabriel García Márquez. When I went to Colombia with
Apichatpong Weerasethakul to make the film *Memoria* it was
so familiar. Like I had been there before. Of course I had,
with Márquez. Since I was fifteen, when I hadn't even taken
in that it was particularly Colombia he was describing. But
all the ghosts were walking still, and taking their place.

Tilda's list makes me think about a few more topics to be discussed in
the future. Some of them would be the ways in which certain books
are laid inside us and how we carry them with us all our lives. Also,
we could explore the reasons we skip pages in books and why they
have lost our attention. Most of all I am thinking about *The Prime of
Miss Jean Brodie* and how to adapt it for the big screen. When Timothy
Snyder's book, *On Tyranny*, as recommended by Tilda, arrives two
days later, I randomly open it to page 71.

The line on this page reads: 'Post-truth is pre-fascism.'

DEBORAH LEVY is the author of acclaimed novels, short stories and plays. She has written
for the Royal Shakespeare Company and dramatised Freud's two most iconic case histories
for the BBC, 'Dora' and 'The Wolf Man'. Her novels *Swimming Home* (2011), *Hot Milk* (2016)
and *The Man Who Saw Everything* (2019) were nominated for the Booker Prize. *The Cost of
Living* and *Things I Don't Want to Know*, translated by Céline Leroy in France, won the Prix
Femina étranger 2020. *Real Estate*, the final volume of her 'living autobiography' trilogy, was
awarded the Christopher Isherwood Prize for Autobiographical Prose, 2022. Her latest novel
is *August Blue*. Levy is a Fellow of the Royal Society of Literature.

# Added Context

A condensed guide to the authors in Tilda's text message.

## GEORGE ELIOT
Nuneaton, 1819 – London, 1880
Author of *Middlemarch*, a book that many essentially marry. The novelist had an interesting life with lots of love affairs. 'Our thoughts are often worse than we are.' Other fans: Stephen Hawking, Martha Stewart, Constance Wu.

## ELIZABETH TAYLOR
Berkshire, 1912 – Buckinghamshire, 1975
The novelist, not the actress, though some readers think that the actress makes a cameo in *Mrs Palfrey at the Claremont*. 'The problem with people who have no vices is that generally you can be pretty sure they're going to have some pretty annoying virtues.' Other fans: Jilly Cooper, Hilary Mantel, François Ozon.

## EVELYN WAUGH
London, 1903 – Somerset, 1966
Depicter of the riotously outrageous in novels such as *Brideshead Revisited*. Wrote good travel books as well. 'Sometimes, I feel the past and the future pressing so hard on either side that there's no room for the present at all.' Other fans: David Bowie, Richard Dawkins, Larry Kramer.

## MARGARET DRABBLE
Sheffield, 1939
Writer of nineteen novels, as well as biographies, literary histories and a personal memoir about jigsaws. 'Perhaps the rare and simple pleasure of being seen for what one is compensates for the misery of being it.' Other fans: Aaron Ayscough, Joyce Carol Oates, Sally Rooney.

## GRAHAM GREENE
Hertfordshire, 1904 – Vevey, Switzerland, 1991
Literary but with a moreish popular touch. Famous novels include *Our Man in Havana*, *Brighton Rock*, and *The End of the Affair*. 'Most things disappoint till you look deeper.' Other fans: Anthony Bourdain, Pete Buttigieg, Colin Firth.

## JOHN BERGER
London, 1926 – Paris, 2017
Art critic, painter and poet. His celebrated *Ways of Seeing* inspired a lot of titles with the format Ways of [insert gerund]. 'What any true painting touches is an absence — an absence of which without the painting, we might be unaware.' Other fans: Geoff Dyer, Emily Ratajkowski, Susan Sontag.

## P. G. WODEHOUSE
Surrey, 1881 – New York, 1975
Pelham Grenville Wodehouse. Lode star of a certain kind of English wit. Best known for his books about gentleman Bertie Wooster and his wise butler Jeeves. 'Success comes to a writer, as a rule, so gradually that it is always something of a shock to him to look back and realise the heights to which he has climbed.' Other fans: Hugh Laurie, Nigella Lawson, Stephen Fry.

## HAFIZ
Shiraz, 1325 – Shiraz, 1390
Persian lyric poet whose work is hugely revered, especially in Iran. His tomb is in the beautiful Mufalla Gardens. 'A day of silence can be a pilgrimage in itself.' Other fans: Ralph Waldo Emerson, Goethe, Friedrich Nietzsche.

## JAMES SALTER
New Jersey, 1925 – New York, 2015
Jet fighter pilot who became a writer, most famously of the novel *A Sport and a Pastime*, an unreliably-narrated story with many sex scenes. 'There is no complete life. There are only fragments. We are born to have nothing, to have it pour through our hands.' Other fans: Rafael de Cárdenas, Teju Cole, Richard Ford.

## CHINUA ACHEBE
Ogidi, Nigeria, 1930 – Boston, 2013
Possibly the greatest Nigerian writer of all time. Famous above all for his first novel, 1958's *Things Fall Apart*, set in a village in the Niger Delta. 'To me, being an intellectual doesn't mean knowing about intellectual issues; it means taking pleasure in them.' Other fans: Chimamanda Ngozi Adichie, Chrissie Hynde, Lin-Manuel Miranda.

## LEO TOLSTOY
Yasnaya Polyana, Russia, 1828 – Lev Tolstoi, Russia, 1910
The author of *War and Peace* was an advocate for nonviolent resistance, whose ideas inspired both Mahatma Gandhi and Martin Luther King Jr. 'Rummaging in our souls, we often dig up something that ought to have lain there unnoticed.' Other fans: David Copperfield, Karl Ove Knausgaard, Rufus Wainwright.

## ANTON CHEKHOV
Taganrog, Russia, 1860 – Badenweiler, Germany, 1904
Playwright who defined what modernism in theatre could mean. 'If you say in the first chapter that there is a rifle hanging on the wall, in the second or third chapter it absolutely must go off.' Other fans: Kazuo Ishiguro, Leila Slimani, Bruce Springsteen.

## WALTER BENJAMIN
Berlin, 1892 – Catalonia, 1940
Perennially relevant philosopher and cultural critic. See his essay 'The Work of Art in the Age of Mechanical Reproduction'. 'There is no document of civilization that is not at the same time a document of barbarism.' Other fans: Greta Gerwig, Dan Graham, Elif Shafak.

## GABRIEL GARCÍA MÁRQUEZ
Aracataca, Colombia, 1927 – Mexico City, 2014
Nobel Prize-winning author of *One Hundred Years of Solitude* and *Love in the Time of Cholera*. Sometimes known simply as Gabo or Gabito. Other fans: Richard E. Grant, Mike Leigh, Kehinde Wiley.

Fred Boissonnas, Bibliothèque de Genève

# THE HAPPY
# READER

# The ODYSSEY today

Bookish Magazine — Issue n° 19

Tell me, Muse, the story
of that resourceful man...

O Muse, sing to me of the man
full of resources...

Sing to me of the man, Muse,
the man of twists and turns...

Tell me about a
complicated man...

Tell me, O Muse, of the Shifty,
the man who wandered afar...

# THE TRUEST FANTASY ever written is about a missing man trying to get home from, and to, a Greek island. This issue's Book of the Season *The Odyssey*, here introduced by SEB EMINA, is the perfect read for slow summer journeys, outbound or inbound.

These lines on the left are all the same. They're the first words of *The Odyssey* — ἄνδρα μοι ἔννεπε, μοῦσα, πολύτροπον, ὃς μάλα πολλὰ, give or take — as understood by five of the people who have translated it. Everyone translates *The Odyssey* in their own way. To have done so initiates you into a special club, where strange things might happen. Like how, when E. V. Rieu whiled away the Second World War completing a new English version, the result was the creation of Penguin Classics.

Those lines all have that mythical ring to them: sailing close to the wind of boring yet so self-serious it is hard to look away. They're as heavy as a block of marble, as ominous as an old ruin someone's taken you to for reasons you must have been told at some point but have embarrassingly forgotten. Except *The Odyssey* then comes to life, which a ruin never does (and even if it did, it would just be merchants selling cloth or something). The 'man of twists and turns' is Odysseus, King of Ithaca, husband of Penelope. That much we guessed. Odysseus is always preceded by his reputation. As we read on, we learn he hasn't been seen for twenty years, not since the aftermath of the Trojan War. Nobody is sure if he is alive or dead. His son, Telemachus, sets off to investigate.

An unsolved mystery, the promise of a journey, the longing of child for parent: it's a good set-up. Then, as with many epics, *The Odyssey* seems to occupy both a greater and lesser amount of time than the duration of the action portrayed. If you take into account flashbacks and side-stories — and much of the book consists of compelling anecdotes delivered at banquets — the story encompasses something between sixty and eighty years. A single lifetime. But it feels like, and most probably is, what happens when a seafaring civilization takes its best stories and embellishes them repeatedly, fifty or a hundred thousand times. *The Odyssey* was written between 700 and 800 BC, but it is also the work of centuries, transmitted and refined by generations of bards.

Why not become a bard yourself? Read it out loud with a friend. What's eleven hours in return for the nourishment of species memory? It'll be your own remake. The remakes never stop: is an artistic milieu even real until it's fed *The Odyssey* through itself? It's what James

**CLASSIC OF CLASSICS**
—
The first Penguin Classics edition of *The Odyssey* was a new translation by E. V. Rieu, an academic outsider who'd prepared it to a backdrop of air raid sirens, bombing raids and the watchful dread of wartime London. 'Something important has happened,' reported *Reynold's News*, upon its publication in 1946. 'There is a new translation of *The Odyssey*, a very contemporary translation, and it costs only one shilling. This is revolutionary.' It went on to sell over three million copies.

Joyce did on behalf of modernist fiction, and it's what New Jersey band Symphony X did for progressive metal. Odyssean cameos are part of the joy of a Mediterranean holiday. A few years ago, on the island of Naxos, I walked up to a cave where the god Zeus, a major *Odyssey* player, is meant to have been born. Why this cave? Who was actually born here? Nobody else was around.

The cave was dark, in a way that seemed immune to the light of my phone. You don't believe it, but you do.

Is *The Odyssey* really a book at all? Is Stonehenge a sculpture park? When things reach a certain age, they become something else. 'Bohemian Rhapsody', Levi's jeans, Robin Day furniture, the game Scrabble: these things get blithely described as

'timeless' quite often. It's guaranteed *The Odyssey* will outlast them, and all their future equivalents as well.

SEB EMINA is editor-in-chief of *The Happy Reader*. He continues to write *Happy Readings*, the free monthly newsletter connected to this magazine (subscribe at thehappyreader.com/newsletter). For updates on other projects, look to Instagram and his personal platform, sebemina.com.

# TO HUNT DOWN HOMER in the Kingdom of Yugoslavia, by JUSTIN E. H. SMITH. The strange life of Milman Parry, an adventuring classicist who upended everything we know about the author of *The Odyssey*.

In 1933 a young, thin, somewhat bird-faced man, with round glasses and a well-trimmed moustache, said the appropriate goodbyes to his wife and two small children at home in Cambridge, Massachusetts, and set out on a voyage to the remotest corners of the Balkans. Once there, he hoped to find the answer to a mystery that was very remote in time and still somewhat  in place from the Kingdom of Yugoslavia in the interwar period: what, namely, is the true origin of literature?

We generally take the prose novel to be the most paradigmatic expression of the literary arts, even if we grant poetry a special place alongside prose, in part in view of its seniority. Poetry came before prose, but how long before? We have the great works  of Homer from the eighth century BCE and not many surviving traces before that. But what if the works of Homer are themselves just the late-arriving transcriptions of a tradition that existed already for centuries as a strictly oral art-form? But if poems were oral traditions before they were written down, how would we know? Our bird-faced man may have landed on an answer.

There are tremendous differences from one culture to another, and exceptions to every generalisation, yet nonetheless we may say on the whole that cultures without written literature place a higher value on memorisation than literate or textual cultures. What is sometimes controversially called 'oral literature' — the vast bodies of epic poetry that various cultures around the world have transmitted across the generations without ever writing them down — includes numerous features that only make sense if you understand them as part of the technical apparatus of constructing a vast mental corpus with no textual counterpart. Notably, heavy reliance on alliteration and epithets — oft-repeated short phrases that express a characteristic feature of the person or thing in question — is a common feature of oral epic traditions throughout the world.

Such epics were not in the first place composed with any intention of seeing them translated into textual form. And so, often, when they finally are written down, they continue to bear the marks of their earlier life as an oral art-form. We have witnessed this process of textualisation of many oral epic traditions in the modern period. The Sundiata epic of the Malinke people, describing heavily mythologised historical events that took place in the Mali Empire in the thirteenth century, was transcribed first into Arabic, and then, by the end of the nineteenth century, was published in French editions compiled by colonial administrators. The Olonkho tradition of the Sakha or Yakut people of north-eastern Siberia only began to be recorded in the early twentieth century, when Polish and Russian ethnologists, and a good number of penal colonists turned ethnologist as a way to bide their time, began to notice the extraordinary feats of memory and recitative endurance of which a certain class of Sakha bards, the *olonkhosuttor*, were capable. And around the same time a similar tradition in the Balkans was beginning to attract the same sort of outside interest: that of the so-called *guslari*, or Bosniak bards, who sing epic tales while playing on the single-stringed *gusle*. Though in this case the most significant researcher of the tradition was not a colonial administrator or a penal colonist, but one

Milman Parry — the same man we have already observed bidding farewell to his family — a Harvard classicist turned ethnomusicologist, travelling on a grant from the Rockefeller Foundation. Although oral narrative traditions have many traits in common wherever they are found, circumstance brought Parry to the Balkans, and not to Siberia, or West Africa, or anywhere else human beings have held society and the generations together by telling epic tales — which is to say, more or less everywhere.

The *guslari* and the *olonkhosuttor*, and their counterparts throughout the world, are, in terms of social hierarchy, rather lowly characters — typically elderly, toothless, with wispy silver hair and ragged clothing; just looking at pictures of them one senses one can smell their breath. They often do not have particularly beautiful voices. There is little in their performance that seems, on the face of it, to be held in common with the lofty and high-status epic-poetic traditions that have been passed down to us in written form from classical Greek and Roman antiquity. And yet, if you look at your transcription closely, you might notice that the features of today's Bosniak or Sakha or Malinke epic share at least certain

*A singer with his gusle*

elementary formulae with those most monumental contributions to the history of Western literature – *The Odyssey* and *The Iliad* of Homer.

The author, or authors, of these latter texts is surely lost forever in the dark abyss of time. We cannot know who Homer was, or who the many generations of Homers were whom we collectively call by that name. But if we want to get some idea of what it may have been like to be there at 'Western' literature's genesis, we could probably do no better than to visit a Balkan bard and listen to his hours-long wedding song. This was Parry's central insight.

Born in Oakland, California, in 1902, Parry received his first degrees at Berkeley. In 1924 he moved from there to study in the philology faculty at the Sorbonne, where four years later he completed a doctoral dissertation entitled *L'épithète traditionnelle dans Homère* [*The Traditional Epithet in Homer*]. Here he began to articulate what would come to be known as the 'Oral Formulaic Hypothesis', a then-controversial theory of the oral origins of Homeric epic. Before Parry, it was generally supposed that there was a single historical figure, a man named Homer, who was a great poet, and who composed *The Odyssey* and *The Iliad* more or less in the form we have them today. But Parry's theory suggests that the familiar epithets so many of us know — 'rosy-fingered dawn', 'many-counselled Odysseus', 'the wine-dark  sea', the last of which would be satirised by James Joyce as 'the snotgreen sea, the scrotumtightening sea' — can only make sense if we understand them as part of the scaffolding of a vast art of memory — and, not just of memory, but, as we'll see soon, an art of creativity as well. The epithets are there not just to ornament, but to help the bard who must master the formal elements required for the marathons of recitation that are his life's calling. And if Homer's works were originally bodies of oral poetry that were transmitted among bards through a complicated arsenal of mnemonic techniques, this almost certainly compels us to suppose that the written work we know today came into existence considerably later than the oral tradition from which the written work derives.

Little in Parry's French classical education under the direction of the great linguist Antoine Meillet, himself a student of the structural linguist Ferdinand de Saussure, could have helped us to predict how his career would develop from there. Once back in the United States, Parry obtained a post in the classics department at Harvard, and became acquainted there with the young classicist Albert Lord (1912–91). A decade  Parry's junior, Lord would go on to make various important contributions to research on the oral poetic tradition of the Balkan *guslari*, who into the twentieth century were spinning out poems with many thousands of lines telling the epic history of the 1389 Battle of Kosovo, and of the great showdown at that site between the Ottoman Sultan Murad I and the Serbian Prince Lazar. From 1933 to 1935 Lord and Parry spent the greater part of two years travelling through Serbia and Montenegro, to the remotest rural locations they could find, where epic tradition still survived largely uncorrupted. Their greatest discovery  was of a humble *guslar* by the name of Avdo Međedović (1875–1955), a Slavicised Albanian Muslim whose recitation of a 12,000-line poem entitled

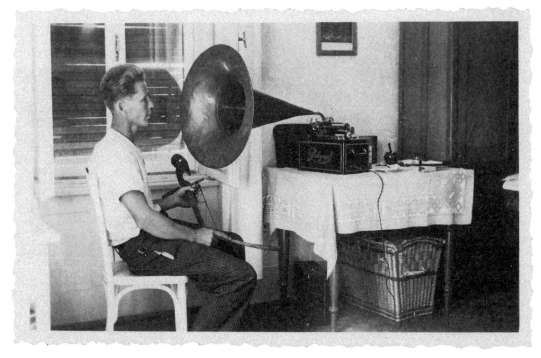

*Parry received much in the way of assistance from a singer named Nikola Vujnović,*
*here seen making a parlograph recording in Dubrovnik, Croatia*

Photographs used with the permission of the Milman Parry Collection of Oral Literature, Harvard University

*The Wedding of Smailagić Meho* would come to serve as the centrepiece of their collection.

Parry and Lord were pioneers in the use of phonographic recording devices in the field, thus paving the way for subsequent generations of ethnomusicologists such as Mieczyslaw Kolinski in Poland, and Alan Lomax and Charles Seeger (father of Pete) in the United States. Lomax and Seeger in particular were interested in folk-musical traditions as the lifeblood of culture passed down across the generations through techniques deeper than language. They saw the study of these traditions as a key part of the project of bringing to light the true parity of all human cultures, as against the hierarchised ladder of relatively more and less advanced cultures that had predominated since the Enlightenment. But Parry is largely unique in seeking to establish the equality of literary forms, textual and oral, 'high' and 'low', in a long-sweeping historical perspective that includes the canonical works of the 'Western' canon alongside the living traditions of oral recitation.

In these living traditions, it is not quite correct to see works as fixed sequences of lines that are memorised word for word. Rather, although the story is known in advance, as are the formal constraints on how it may be told, nonetheless the singular works are to a certain extent 'spontaneously generated' each time a bard sets about reciting them — much

like the 'freedom within constraints' that is often invoked to characterise improvisation in both the jazz and the Indian raga traditions. The formulae in the Oral Formulaic Hypothesis are therefore not so much scaffold as building blocks, adjustable pieces that can be rearranged and built upon each time anew. Transcription or phonographic recording freezes one such version in time, and typically turns it into the canonical and 'correct' version, but when it gets frozen, and in which particular arrangement, is a highly contingent matter. As Lord would later put it, '[A]n oral poem is not composed *for* but *in* performance'; and this must have been the case as much for Homer as for the living, breathing bards whose art the pair of researchers were busy laying down on wax. As Parry wrote excitedly after hearing one of Međedović's recitations: '[One] has the overwhelming sense that he is, in some way, hearing Homer.'

Lord had a long career, which largely consisted of the development of certain promising insights in the work of his former partner, culminating notably in

a book called *The Singer of Tales* in 1960.  If these strands remained only promises in the work of Parry himself, this is because his life was cut short, in the Palms Hotel in downtown Los Angeles at the age of thirty-three, with a gunshot. He had carried a pistol with him during his Balkan travels, for protection, he said, from bandits. On 3 December 1935, after arriving in his hometown with his wife, and checking into their room, the same gun that had accompanied him on his voyages went off, and put a bullet in his heart. The coroner called it an accident, claiming the gun discharged inad-

 vertently as Parry removed it from his suitcase. But this determination did not satisfy everyone, including the Parrys' own daughter, who accused her mother of murder. Others say it was suicide, and others still suspect foul play on the part of a nefarious group of people who had been defrauding his mother-in-law of her wealth, which had been the precipitating crisis for the young couple's return to California.

When I try to picture the scene, I see the hotel in the Coen Brothers' *Barton Fink*: an attempt at elegance in a place far too sunny for it, far too golden: 1930s LA, so bright it's noir. Everything seems covered in dust, though the hotel is not  yet old, and the whole city seems haunted by the recent past its hasty construction has only imperfectly concealed. Such a different landscape than the Balkans, shaped by such different historical forces. And yet guns work the same in each.

In his death, it is as if Parry entered the bloodstream of the legends he dedicated his life to understanding. He could have died old, too, but that would have been less compelling, as far as legends go. It is almost as if he wished to illustrate for us just how great the gap is between the length of art and the shortness of life. If the bards were not mortals, their epics could go on to infinity.

JUSTIN E. H. SMITH is the author of seven books, most recently *The Internet Is Not What You Think It Is: A History, A philosophy, A warning*. He is currently co-translating a Siberian work of oral epic poetry, in the Olonkho tradition of the Sakha people. Like a certain Greek epic hero, he sometimes prefers to go by the name of 'Nobody'.

FOOD

# A VERY OLD SAUSAGE was a very nice treat, and other sausage trivia, in this illuminating article by food writer REBECCA MAY JOHNSON. Sausages are so archetypal that they've attracted the attention of psychoanalysts, who seem suspicious about making them but not so much about eating them.

'There are at least three words in Greek for a sausage...'

When browsing the food section of antiquarian stalwart Edinburgh Books this summer, I was delighted to read the words 'The Sausage in Antiquity', in the 1953 collection *Food* by André Simon. An instant purchase! Simon's essay is stuffed with tasty offcuts of ancient sausage trivia. As a socialist sausage enthusiast, I was thrilled to find out about political comedy *The Knights* by Aristophanes, in which a sausage-seller (and maker) saves the Athenian people from a warmongering leader who exploits his subjects:

CLEON:
What makes you so bold as to dare to speak to my face?

SAUSAGE-SELLER: Because I know both how to speak and how to cook.

The sausage-seller has a gross-out comic tongue and the culinary ingenuity inherent in his wares, and these are the qualities that become his tools of battle: 'And I will pull out your arse to stuff like a sausage!' he cries. Making sausages teaches the sausage-seller, Agoracritus, all he needs to know in order to overthrow a tyrant. Among other titbits, Simon also

1. ARISTOPHANES
—
The most important playwright working in a form known as Old Comedy, the origins of which some think are traceable to the Komos, a form of drunken procession in Ancient Greece, notable for its phallic songs.

relays the strange vision of an ancient sausage-led welfare practice where, 'in frugal Sparta, sausages were nailed to the wall in order that old gentlemen might come and take a bite at them when hungry.' The common sausage will feed the people!

My recent preoccupation with everything sausage-related came after reading the 1970 paper 'Living Creatively' by psychoanalyst D. W. Winnicott, in which he writes that following a recipe for cooking sausages could teach him nothing but slavish compliance. I was deeply irritated. Winnicott uses a sausage recipe as a case study to define what it is to live creatively: he says you can either follow a recipe for cooking sausages and get 'nothing' from the experience or encounter them 'as if for the first time' and feel 'original'.

Outrageous! Because, quite apart from Aristophanes' many ways with sausages in *The Knights* in 424 BC, Homer imparts a recipe for sausages in *The Odyssey*, in 800 BC, almost 3,000 years ago. There is no way Winnicott could even breathe air free from a recipe for cooking sausages: we are practically *steeped* in sausage recipes. In a potent rhetorical gesture, Homer gives us a recipe for sausages and a metaphor for sexual jealousy:

So he forced his spirit into submission,
the rage in his breast reined back —
      unswerving,
all endurance. But he himself kept tossing,
      turning,
intent as a cook before some white-hot
      blazing fire
who rolls his sizzling sausage back and forth,

packed with fat and blood — keen to broil it
quickly,
tossing, turning it, this way, that way — so
he cast about:
how could he get these shameless suitors in
his clutches,
one man facing a mob?

Homer shows us that sausages are filled with blood
and fat, that they need to be rotated to cook evenly,

and that sausages are life-filled, ripe for metaphor
and impart self-knowledge, as well as being for
eating.
And so: *cook a sausage!*
I like them cooked with grapes, onions, white
wine and vinegar at this time of year...

REBECCA MAY JOHNSON's book
*Small Fires, an Epic in the Kitchen* is described by *The Sunday Times* as 'a manifesto
for reclaiming cooking as an intellectual'.

OP-ED

# THE POPULAR ONE-EYED MONSTER
and his warning to us now, by NICHOLAS
JUBBER. Scary yet sweet, and anything but
simple: that's the Cyclops.

One eye, as big as the mouth below, which gapes
open in a monstrous scowl. This is Polyphemus, the
Cyclops, the most iconic and the most universally
reimagined of the enemies faced by Odysseus. I've
encountered the Cyclops in a variety of places: in
his legendary home in Sicily, for example, his face
protruded from a pizzeria and his name from B&Bs
and other businesses, while bathers swam amongst
the basaltic rocks he's said to have hurled against the
escaping Greeks. I've listened to his story in Athens,
recited by members of the public in the Archaeolog-
ical Museum, while a prominent musician accompanied them on the lyre. And, like most of us, I've
been confronted with variations of his distinctive
glare in the stories I've consumed throughout my
life, new or old, in books or on screens.

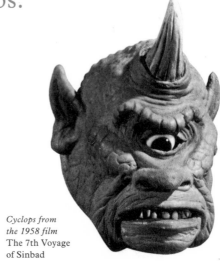

*Cyclops from
the 1958 film*
The 7th Voyage
of Sinbad

© Alamy

The one-eyed giant is a striking image. Folklor-
ic variations across the world underline his status
as an archetype, from Bungisngis, the 'giggling
giant' of the Philippines, outwitted by a cunning
monkey's gift of a belt (which turns out to be a
boa constrictor), to the medieval Turkic tale of
*Dede Korkut*, in which a horse-riding hero called
Basat gouges out a one-eyed giant's eye with a
red-hot spit — a scene strikingly similar to Odysseus' defeat of the Cyclops but reimagined in the
bow-shooting, verse-chanting spirit of the steppe.
Consistent to these encounters is that the single
eye isn't a weakness, it's a massive, powerful organ,

evoking the fiery glare of the sun, projecting single-
mindedness and ferocious intensity of purpose.
Monsters evolve, yet certain motifs, certain visual
codes, remain intact. For ancient audiences, monsters evoked their fears of the wild places around
them, of unknown peoples from across the sea. For
Odysseus, the Cyclopes — Polyphemus' people —
were 'lawless brutes' who represented the wild ter-
rain the Greeks sought to tame. But other works
treated the Cyclopes more respectfully. Classical
poets such as Hesiod depicted them as master crafts-
men, the artisans behind the magical thunderbolt
wielded by Zeus or Poseidon's trident, albeit with

a demeanour characterised by strength and force. Homer stripped away the craftsmanship, retaining only what Hesiod called their 'very violent hearts'. In *The Odyssey*, the Cyclops's man-eating gluttony is moderated only by the pathos of his — admittedly quite sweet — care for his sheep.

Here we can glimpse a moment of transition: the mighty demigod, worthy of our respect, reduced, for narrative purposes, to a monster to be reviled. But when Polyphemus the Cyclops invokes revenge from his father, Poseidon, god of the sea, we see how fluid and incomplete that transition remains. And it flows all the way to the present day. The Cyclopes remain at large, only now evoking contemporary anxieties. No longer do we see our giants as gods, or as representatives of the natural world, for we have killed off one and tamed the other (or so we like to think), but in doing so we have created another force whose power frightens us just as much. We call it by the same ancient Greek word used to describe the craft of the Cyclopes: *techne*, 'technology'.

At first glance, there's an insurmountable gulf between the ancient Cyclopes, hammering iron on their enormous anvils in the caves of Mount Etna, and modern-day sci-fi visions of robots with single eye-stalks or LED lights sweeping across the corridor of a space station. But one-eyed giants, as it turns out, are not only visions of the past but also prophecies of the future. The Cylons of TV series *Battlestar Galactica*, relentlessly hunting down humans, or the giant robot Shockwave in the *Transformers* franchise, its face little more than a fiery red glow: these sci-fi giants carry off the monocular look with the same intensity as their ancient predecessors.

The homage can be explicit (see He-Man's occasional antagonist, Tri-klops, or the diving thief in cult children's cartoon *Spongebob Squarepants*, known literally as 'Cyclops') or it can be subtle, but whether or not it's conscious is beside the point. Homer, after all, was tweaking an established model. The ancient Greeks saw a single-eyed giant as representing a twin capacity for violence and craftsmanship, and many of our one-eyed robo-villains today replicate the same combination. The decepticon Shockwave is a genius scientist, while the Cylons have built an advanced society, including, in the 2004 remake, their own monotheistic religion.

Here is a lesson that spans the millennia: behind these images of terror there are complicated cultures that we should strive to understand. Odysseus is punished for failing to see Polyphemus as anything more than a monster; and for ten years his journey is lashed by the wrath of the monster's divine father. His nemesis, it turns out, is more than a 'lawless brute'. And sci-fi iterations today pour out similar ambiguities. Go to war with the giants, by all means, but don't underestimate them. For one eye, fitted to bulk, has a lethal impact, and whichever end of the historical spectrum the Cyclops is coming from, it can only be defeated by the wiliest of heroes.

NICHOLAS JUBBER is the author of five books about history and travel, including *Epic Continent*, about his journey from Greece to Iceland in the wake of Europe's epic tales. His latest book is *The Fairy Tellers*.

---

THEATRE

# AN ODYSSEAN EVENT in Amsterdam caught the attention of ELIOT HAWORTH. After his visit he sent the following short report.

On a hot afternoon a group of eight theatregoers met in a former shipyard in Amsterdam-Noord. A raised wooden walkway snaked its way through a densely planted urban forest dotted with the carcasses of old houseboats that had been repurposed into a variety of shared workspaces and mixed-use creative studios. The group had gathered for a rendition of *The Odyssey* that was to be enacted over the course of an hour-long walk.

The party set off on a path fringed with dense

2. SIRENS

Contrary to popular belief, the song of the sirens isn't irresistible due to the quality of their voices but because they promise information, that Odysseus is desperate to know, if only he'd go over and see them.

foliage and drooping tree branches. With each corner rounded they encountered another of the epic's important, but often overlooked, women: the sorceress Circe, Odysseus' mother Anticlea, the sirens, the nymph Calypso and the princess Nausicaa. The mood was relaxed and convivial. On the short journeys between storytellers, the guests stopped to pick blackberries, discuss the finer points of the last dramatic interlude and take photos of the afternoon sun reflecting off the river IJ. For the final leg of the expedition the show's director, Marie Phillips, took on the role of Odysseus' wife, Penelope, as several audience members settled back on a wooden bench and closed their eyes.

Odysseus is away. He has been for twenty years. Through all that time Penelope has stayed at home and waited. She is a queen and a mother. She can't just set off on a boat into the great unknown. She has a kingdom to look after and

a son to raise. One day she wakes to silence. It's the first time in years that her home, usually filled with huge, hairy, sweaty, stinking men, has been quiet. She gets up, goes downstairs. The smell hits her first. The smell of iron and piss and shit. The smell of death. She walks into the great hall. There's blood everywhere, bodies everywhere. One man stands in the middle of it all. Odysseus. Of course it's Odysseus. Penelope stands there in the blood of the dead, looking at her husband. Home at last.

After the applause, the audience walked the remainder of the wooden walkway and emerged from the secluded garden. Outside the quiet was broken by the sound of afternoon revellers at a nearby bar-slash-restaurant-slash-swimming spot. People were lounging in swimwear, chatting loudly and drinking fun cocktails. The audience went its separate ways. Calypso, Penelope and Nausicaa went for a pizza.

ELIOT HAWORTH is a writer and editor from London. He was in Amsterdam while working on the 36th issue of *Fantastic Man* magazine.

FASHION

# TROJAN HORSEMEN have finally breached the gateways to creative power, by JEREMY LEWIS. What's the best way to understand the legacy of Virgil Abloh, entrepreneur, fashion designer and all-round creative alchemist? By considering the classical metaphor plastered across the merch at his final museum show.

Fashion is neither artifice nor lustrous veneer. It is in fact a deep well of egos and personalities, dreams and ambitions, triumphs and failures, myths and legends. If we scry into its reflective surface, it will often reveal to us the truth. If we stand before it and make a wish, that wish might even come true.

The story of the late designer Virgil Abloh is the stuff modern myths are made of. He was born and raised in the American Midwest to Ghanaian

immigrant parents. He studied civil engineering and architecture and eventually worked for Kanye West as his creative right hand (the significance of which is marred by West's later leap from grace). Abloh was called the 'ultimate multi-hyphenate', which is a newfangled way of saying 'Renaissance man'. Indeed, he worked across a host of creative disciplines, including music, art and most notably fashion. He founded the label Off-White and commanded the attention of the luxury industry's movers and shakers with his uncanny ability to keep in lockstep with the mercurial spirit of the times. Abloh was a Pied Piper ensorcelling a new generation of consumers, an alchemist able to transmute culture into desirable, saleable goods. In 2018 he was hired as artistic director of Louis Vuitton's men's ready-to-wear. Although Abloh was not the first designer of colour to take the top job at a conglomerate-owned luxury house (many are quick to forget Oswald Boateng's stint at Givenchy), his appointment was nonetheless unparalleled and auspicious. Its profoundness reverberated not only through fashion but through all its adjacent cultural spheres. And then tragically in 2021, at the young age of forty-one, Abloh was gone. A victim of cardiac angiosarcoma.

In the wake of his death, the communities Abloh inhabited have sought to reconcile and articulate his loss. One of the most poignant expressions of Abloh's legacy is a phrase coined by his friend and collaborator Tremaine Emory: 'the sunroof of the Trojan Horse'. It has become a maxim that Abloh's friends and admirers have espoused and rallied behind, so much so that it adorned commemorative T-shirts, jeans and hoodies for Abloh's retrospective exhibition, *Figures of Speech*, when it was staged at the Brooklyn Museum in 2022. More than the actual title of the show, it has become synonymous with Abloh's body of work: a credo to be taken up and brandished by all his true believers.

'The sunroof of the Trojan Horse' is of course a reference to the wooden horse first mentioned in Homer's *Iliad* and discussed at several points in *The Odyssey*, before permeating through classical Greek and Roman literature and into our modern lexicon. Virgil's (no relation to Abloh) later epic poem *The Aeneid* tells the story in detail: the great hero Odysseus and his band of soldiers hide within its bowels and trick the Trojans into accepting it as a victory trophy. Once inside the city walls, Odysseus springs out, opens the city gates to the Greeks and thus ends the Trojan War. As a metaphor, it speaks to the covert tactics people of colour have had to use to gain entry into spaces where they historically have not been invited or welcomed. In this instance, it specifically refers to Abloh's ascent into the upper echelons of fashiondom and the paradigm shift and opportunities for other people of colour that it created.

Emory's Trojan Horse has layers, one of which is the dynamic of combative and opposing forces, a conflict between 'us' and 'them'. It's a dynamic familiar to many minorities and 'others' who have found themselves spurned or threatened by the mainstream yet with no choice, for the sake of survival and posterity, to participate in it. The struggle for a seat at the table is real. Another layer is a sense of time. The Trojan War was a long and arduous campaign. Emory's horse represents the culmination of its own epic saga; a single act of cunning that is in fact the sum total of the many who came and battled before. Emory's Trojan Horse also has a sunroof. This addition adds levity but also essential

3. TREMAINE EMORY
—
The Atlanta-born, Queens-raised founder of influential clothing brand Denim Tears, and, as of 2022, the creative director of Supreme, one of the biggest streetwear brands in the world.

4. TROJAN WAR
—
For many years the war was seen as a fiction, and Troy, the city in which it supposedly took place, as a myth. Now it is generally accepted that Hisarlik, a ruin in modern day Turkey, is Troy, site of the war from which the legend grew.

nuance. It's a repudiation of clandestine activity, of having to lurk in the shadows, as Emory elaborates in an interview with *Complex* magazine:

> We had to sneak in, but we're here now. And more of us are coming in. That's what 'sunroof of the Trojan Horse' means. We letting the fucking top down on this bitch. No more hiding, no more sneaking our friends in. No more any of that. Fully us, fully Black, fully trans, fully gay, fully lesbian, fully whatever you are. Fully you. You're just as viable as anyone else.

The sunroof of the Trojan Horse, or rather the specific moment in fashion that it describes, is likely to be Abloh's most important contribution, even more than his prowess as a designer or his influence on style. It is simultaneously a declaration of what has transpired and a hopeful prediction of what is yet to come. It's an expression of victory as well as aspiration. It is a truth reflected back in the mirror of fashion and a wish whispered to the well. It is a legend in the making that grows, like all great legends do, in the telling.

JEREMY LEWIS is a writer and strategist with a keen interest in fashion history. He was previously the publisher of *Garmento* and has contributed to various titles including *Fantastic Man*, *PIN-UP*, *Encens*, *Artforum*, and *i-D* digital. You can follow his commentary on fashion's past and present on Instagram @lewissmag.

MATERIAL

# GOODBYE, SEA SILK, mystical byproduct of Mediterranean molluscs. At the dreamy studio of the woman who creates these glimmering Odyssean fibres, SABINE MIRLESSE pays witness to a dying craft. But what is provoking the tears of the tourists who make this pilgrimage?

Sea silk, or byssus (etymologically in resonance with the Greek word *bussos*, meaning 'from the depths of the sea'), caught my attention a few years back. Somewhere in my leaning towers of half-read research materials I came upon a mention of a woman on a tiny island off the south coast of Sardinia who dove for it and wove it. Her name was Chiara. She claimed to be a kind of alchemist: the last person on earth who could turn the beard of giant Mediterranean molluscs into a golden thread mentioned in the great sequel to *The Iliad*, and even, she claimed, the Bible itself. The material is subject to conjecture, with a pile of arguments for its Homeric origins and a pile of killjoy counter-claims for the sheer impossibility of its existence. However, the impact of its story I witnessed firsthand. I wrote to her and went to see. What I found were people flocking to her atelier on Sant'Antioco to watch her chant a kind of whale song in a jar full of lemon juice and herbs, drenching the fibres she had collected from the surrounding coast in citrus and prayer, before drying them in the sun. She would weave the treated material on her spindle and it would glisten golden.

*Il Maestro*, as she was referred to locally, took me for a walk along the coast, eventually stopping at sundown before a plunging cliff overlooking a small rocky bay, where below there was a natural pool, like a tiny volcanic crater. It was the sort of place you already know was the site of ancient ablutions, even before you're told. She held the *bisso*, as she called it in Sardo, up against the setting sun, incanted to the waters and bowed to the horizon. She had made a promise to the sea itself never to allow any purchase of the silk, no matter how high the bid, she told me proudly, defiantly, pleased with her decision. Instead she preferred to intuit certain visitor's situations, and would offer a

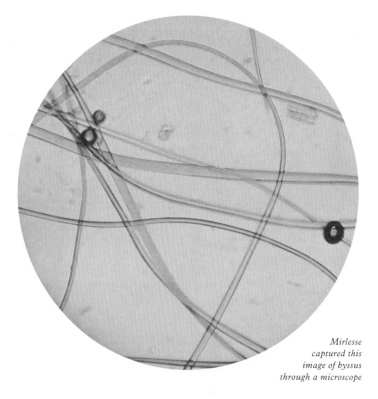

*Mirlesse captured this image of byssus through a microscope*

through water: *L'Oeil véritable de la terre, c'est l'eau.* (The true eye of the earth is water.) If water can see, then we have the possibility of being seers in its presence. I never saw Chiara dive for the material as I'd longed to, but staring down from the back of a boat just before leaving the island it didn't matter at all. I peered into the sea, watching an anchor lowered and then summoned back, its flat, murky silhouette turned into a three-dimensional object, half expecting it to bring up treasure — retrieving some kind of knowledge of that invisible depth. Chiara's story of byssus had spoken to that threshold of invisibility. In mythology, the sea is an access point to the depths of our world and can act as a passageway connecting the heavens and the realm of the dead. Today, nature documentaries remind us that we know about as little of our own ocean floor as we do of outer space. In 2015, Nasa funded the centre for theological inquiry at Princeton to study what the effects of discovery of life on other planets would have on us. Whether submarine or interstellar, the places where we must hold our breaths — that first step to making a wish — are ripe territory for asking and desiring, ingredients for divining but also for little apotropaisms.

There were a pair of sisters in Sant'Antioco who also showed me byssus they had woven into tapestries for the Vatican. Their story was less perfumed with the power of protection and divination. Nothing had been drawn from the surrounding waters and made to make the spindle glow. They had no pact with the sea, but simply acted out their craftsmanship on the fibres of a local shell. There was not a hint of mystery in their explanation. I was happy to have met them, but I preferred Chiara's tale.

length of bracelet, tying it around their wrists. The gift was for those lost or sick, in need of protection or trying to conceive. Tears would often cloud the eyes of these tourist pilgrims. Though visitors were crying nearly every day, to be fair. A longing to believe in the magic of such objects seemed very human. That it should be the stuff of epic texts gave it even more power.

Untreated, the raw nest of fibres that Chiara worked with had a brownish, dark red hue. Were these the 'crimson threads' that Queen Arete is weaving on when Nausicaa arrives to tell her of her strange dream, on the morning of Odysseus' arrival? Irrespective of how it reconciled to the text, I was satisfied with her decision to pull something wine-dark from the sea and transform it into an object she could impart small blessings with (and use to take donations for the atelier). Most left seemingly touched by a seer, a drop of benediction in her offering.

In *L'Eau et les Rêves* (*Water and Dreams*), Gaston Bachelard makes an argument for hydromancy, the art of divination

6. GASTON BACHELARD
—
Best known in English for *The Poetics of Space*, published in 1957. A philosophical meditation on buildings, art and the imagination, the book's chapter headings include 'House and Universe', 'Corners' and 'The Phenomenology of Roundness'.

SABINE MIRLESSE is an artist based in Paris. She once took a voyage in search of the centre of the Mediterranean as part of an *Odyssey*-themed artist residency.

# INTENSELY SEARCHING

01 If Homer really didn't exist then it's amazing his name is still right there on every edition. Perhaps that's just because people are used to it, but there's also something unsettling about a story like that just forming out of the air. It's tempting to call it the cultural equivalent of how a natural wonder such as the Great Coral Reef comes about through a process too gradual for individual lifetimes, or to observe how no individual ant has any real sense of the nest. But there's a more exact parallel in the way AI image generators use all of the pictures our culture has created as a raw mulch from which to conjure new ones. In this sense Homer is not *The Odyssey*'s 'author' but shorthand for an early version of an image generation service like DALL-E, one that didn't need computer circuits but bards as its processor, and had the benefit of centuries of audiences to smooth out the rougher edges. So when we ask DALL-E to produce an image of a 'rosy-fingered dawn', as we have done many times on the right, it is with a feeling that this is as correct and proper a rosy-fingered dawn as has ever been seen, the triangulation of all the billions of pink-tinted sunrises that we as a species have witnessed and shared, like how that phrase itself might have been tweaked and retouched here and there until it created the most perfect possible effect on the gathered crowds who listened, somewhere in the place that became Greece, in a time of which we know little, except that this story was somehow a collaboration between everyone who belonged to it. (See 'To Hunt Down Homer', p.38, for more on *The Odyssey*'s origins).

N 35° 54' 44.64"
E -5° 25' 12.36"

N 40° 47' 28.32"
E 14° 11' 12.84"

N 38° 11' 33.72"
E 15° 33' 27.36"

02 Alternatively, could the real rosy-fingered sunrises and wine-dark seas be located somewhere amid the actual Greek islands of the Mediterranean? How precise are the locations visited by Odysseus, Telemachus and the rest of the cast? Can they be visited? Can they be photographed? Perhaps the most systematic attempt to settle this question occurred in 1912 when Victor Bérard, a French politician obsessed by classical Greece, and Fred Boissonas, a Swiss photographer, went on a months-long journey that claimed to prove through photographs, including the ones on these pages, that *The Odyssey* could be read as a faithful 'geographical document'.

N 41° 15' 03.60"
E 13° 02' 41.99"

32' 24.71"
15' 09.72"

' 20.76"
' 36.24"

N 38° 10' 39.72"
E 20° 29' 16.80"

64"
76"

7' 42.72"
0' 01.91"

N 38° 11' 17.52"
E 15° 33' 41.76"

53

03 Any attempt to seek out the 'real' geography of *The Odyssey* risks smoothing over its other ways of being present. For example, a story about the after-effects of war inevitably chimes with those caught up in conflicts presently taking place. These pages (dated 19 July 2022) are from the daybook of Vladislav Davidzon, former editor-in-chief of *The Odessa Review*, documenting

time spent in the Ukrainian city during the first months of the Russian invasion. Actually, the connection goes deeper than just circumstance. One story as to the origins of Odessa's name has it that Catherine the Great wished for a feminine form of 'Odysseus'. Another links it to a lost Ancient Greek city named Odessos in honour of Homer's hero.

04 In the rest of the world, where the soporific qualities of late capitalism still hold sway, the word 'Odyssey' greets us constantly through the names of consumer products. Such an old and evocative term, yet somehow never behind the times: pure catnip for any marketing professional. No matter what you're selling, whether it's a wetsuit, teapot or home jacuzzi, the implication of daring softened by the centrality of tradition offers a potent springboard from which to shift units. Viewed through this matrix, the book is simply one more product sharing the same name as a Nike trainer.

$179 (used)

Magnavox Odyssey² home video game console
*Named the '21st greatest video game console' by gaming website IGN.*

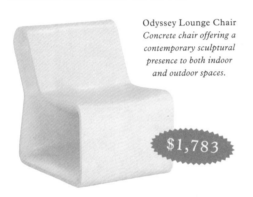

Odyssey Lounge Chair
*Concrete chair offering a contemporary sculptural presence to both indoor and outdoor spaces.*

$1,783

$1.49

Odyssey reduced fat sour cream
*Made with Odyssey Greek yoghurt!*

$42

Odyssey Pinot Noir 2013
*Youthful yet weighty with an elegant fruity ripeness and profound depth of flavour. Cherry, plum and cedar notes.*

$1,530

S. T. Dupont Space Odyssey premium fountain pen
*Writing implement coated in iridescent galactic blue lacquer. Only 2001 pieces available.*

DreamMaker Odyssey Lounger Spa

$5,499

*Enjoy a spa getaway without leaving home for twenty years!*

$87

GoSea Odyssey Men's Wetsuit
*Ideal for watersports.*

£456

Odyssey dual-purpose battery
*More powerful and longer-lasting than conventional marine batteries!*

Entegra Coach Odyssey Motor Home
*The perfect hub for a family adventure, the Odyssey comes with a built-in infotainment centre plus a computer-balanced driveshaft to ensure a smooth ride for all.*

$167,861

PRICE ON REQUEST

Odyssey Monaco LCD watch with Digital Hands
*Boasting a dual time display, countdown timer, light and chronograph.*

Become a commuting hero!

$579

6KU Odyssey 8-Speed City Bicycle
*Combines a high tensile steel frame and classic 8-speed gearing with a sleek aesthetic and eye-catching design, all for a highly affordable price.*

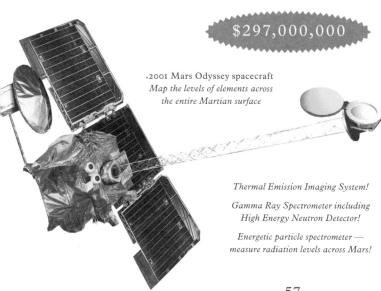

$297,000,000

.2001 Mars Odyssey spacecraft
*Map the levels of elements across the entire Martian surface*

*Thermal Emission Imaging System!*

*Gamma Ray Spectrometer including High Energy Neutron Detector!*

*Energetic particle spectrometer — measure radiation levels across Mars!*

£149

Odyssey DFX Golf Putter
*For an authentic smooth feel.*

£18

AFC Odyssey Teapot
*Australian fine china, 1 litre / 35oz.*

# DIARY OF A FIRST READ bravely embarked upon by author ROB DOYLE while hanging out with his friend, a musician in an unnamed band. Doyle and his friend enhance their reading in various ways. Although they don't forget to have fun between sessions, they can't seem to stop seeing echoes of Homer in the unrelated city of Berlin, Germany.

I began reading *The Odyssey* on a journey home. More accurately, I read not the poem itself but the introduction — nor was I exactly going 'home' either. I was returning to Berlin by train from Paris, where for a heat-stricken fortnight my girlfriend Roisin and I had been minding a friend's cat (and flat) while she was away. We would stay in Germany till the end of summer, then move back to Dublin.

Our friend Lias, likewise engaged in a long game of nomadic musical chairs, met us off the train. He was between recording sessions with his band and for a few weeks we were putting him up in our spare room. More to the point, he was down for Homer. I'd expected a bit of ribbing when I'd suggested reading the great epic aloud together, but he'd surprised me by immediately acceding. We would take it in turns, a chapter each. If we read one or two a day, we just might finish all twenty-four before Lias headed home to London.

We began on the first day of August. I went first, standing in the centre of the spare bedroom in the evening heat. Roisin — the only one among us with an education in the classics and the only one who'd really read *The Odyssey* — stayed for the opening pages before going off to do yoga. I'd taken a look at the epic in my early twenties while making an autodidact's run at the canon, but I had clearer memories of *The Iliad*. In quick recap I told Lias that *The Odyssey* followed on from Homer's earlier blockbuster, in which Achilles led the Greek army in a war against Troy, and picked up the story subsequent to that war. Odysseus was a comrade of Achilles who'd been missing for many years in distant lands.

'Achilles — isn't he the one played by Brad Pitt?'

'Is he?'

'Yeah. In *Troy*.'

'I never saw it, somehow.'

'The film is a wasted opportunity. Odysseus is played by...' He scanned his memory. 'Sean Penn.'

'Sean *Penn*? That doesn't make sense. He's better playing shady lawyers. Odysseus is a warrior.'

'Sean Bean! I always mix them up. Sean Bean.'

The early chapters concern not Odysseus but his son Telemachus, who we first meet on his native island of Ithaca. I read to my audience about young Telemachus' rage as he watches the band of suitors who've been hanging around the family home in his father's absence, trying it on with his mother, Penelope, while 'feasting themselves sick, swilling our glowing wine as if there's no tomorrow'. There are 108 of these suitors, all trying their luck — we can admire their youthful self-confidence even while pointing out that they're not being very realistic about their chances. Lias read the second chapter while reclining on the bed. We'd each eaten a cannabis brownie — there was a Tupperware container full of them in the fridge, a gift from our friend Myriam — and I savoured its effects as Homer's cadences rolled over me like steady, whispering waves from that wine-dark sea. I'd been looking forward to making a puerile quip the first time anybody said 'rosy-fingered

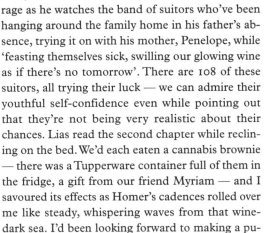

Dawn', but in Robert Fagles' translation it was always 'young Dawn with her rose-red fingers'.

I took over to read the third chapter. Then the exertion of concentrating while baked sent us gladly to our beds, where a deep, kind sleep overcame us.

* * *

The next day we sat in Görlitzer Park, watching the men throwing frisbee like Greeks. When we got home that evening, we voyaged on through Telemachus' last episode in the lead role before Daddy O takes over. There's some great dining in this chapter. Homer never skimps on the details of a banquet or booze-up. The appetiteful phrase 'feasting on sides of meat and drafts of heady wine' gets plenty of use. While everyone fills their bellies, King Menelaus gets to reminiscing for Telemachus' sake about the war and his old comrade-in-arms Odysseus. This sets off much weeping. They're all at it — it's so healthy and candid, none of that northern European repression here.

Now Helen, King Menelaus' wife and the daughter of Zeus — also, let's not forget, the woman whose desirability sparked off the Trojan War — decides to spike her guests' drinks. Into Telemachus and company's wine bowl 'she slipped a drug, heart's-ease, dissolving anger,/ magic to make us all forget our pains'.

'Ketamine,' I said, interrupting my own reading.
'Nah, man, it's not kezzle, it's M-Dizzle.'
I read on:

*No one who drank it deeply, mulled in wine,*
*could let a tear roll down his cheeks that day,*
*not even if his mother should die, his father die...*

'Yeah, that's definitely MDMA,' Lias concluded.

There follows a strange rumour about Odysseus. The great hero, Telemachus learns, is trapped on an island, detained 'in the nymph Calypso's house — she holds him there by force'.

'By force?' Lias wasn't having it. 'He's bedded down with a nymph on her love island and we're meant to believe it's some sort of gender-flipped MeToo scenario? This guy thinks he's a *victim!*'

In the next chapter, Big O takes centre stage as Calypso is ordered by the gods to release her captive sex toy. Before sending him off on a raft, lustrous Calypso bathes her man and treats him to

one last, lasciviously described feast — then fucks his brains out. Like FKA twigs in her brazen song 'Two Weeks', the nymph aims to show him so hot a time that his wife's memory is obliterated under steamy pleasure ('Hardly right, is it,/ for mortal woman to rival immortal goddess?'). Knowing she'll never possess his heart, she contents herself with giving the rest of him sensations he won't easily forget. Withdrawing with him one last time 'into the cavern's deep recesses,/ long in each other's arms they lost themselves in love.'

Homer, which is to say the Greeks, *got* sex, understood it as the basic motivating factor in human existence, without succumbing to prudish, monotheistic moralising. Just about everyone in *The Odyssey* is 'chafing with lust', and no one can let their guard down lest some fit young hero or spunky god seduces their beloved ('Suspicious we are, we men who walk the earth'). In Homer, narrative itself thinks with its dick, and it's this irrepressible horniness of gods and mortals alike that keeps getting his protagonists into dramatically rich hot water. Even the scenery is horny — the shores, forests and enchanted cave of Calypso's island are described in terms that are lusciously moist, enveloping, vaginal.

* * *

To face down yet another heatwave we headed to Teufelssee lake in the Grunewald Forest south of the city. Half of Berlin had thought to get out there and we swam amid nymphs, nudists, pretty girls who stripped off to reveal dangling dicks, and the snakes and *Wildeschweine* of Teufelssee. It was nearly midnight when we returned home to get stuck into the next couple of chapters. *The Odyssey* had become our evening entertainment, the gripping drama series we looked forward to at the end of a hard day's slacking off. This time Lias read first. Being read to is more lulling; you need to stay alert if you're not to drift off into seafaring dreams. As the chapter begins, Odysseus washes up in the land of the Phaeacians looking the worse for wear and is taken care of by the radiant princess Nausicaa. When we first meet her, she is sleeping in a lovely girlish threesome with 'two handmaids fair as the Graces... beside her'. There follows a sultry scene in which Nausicaa and her maids bathe and wash their clothes in the river.

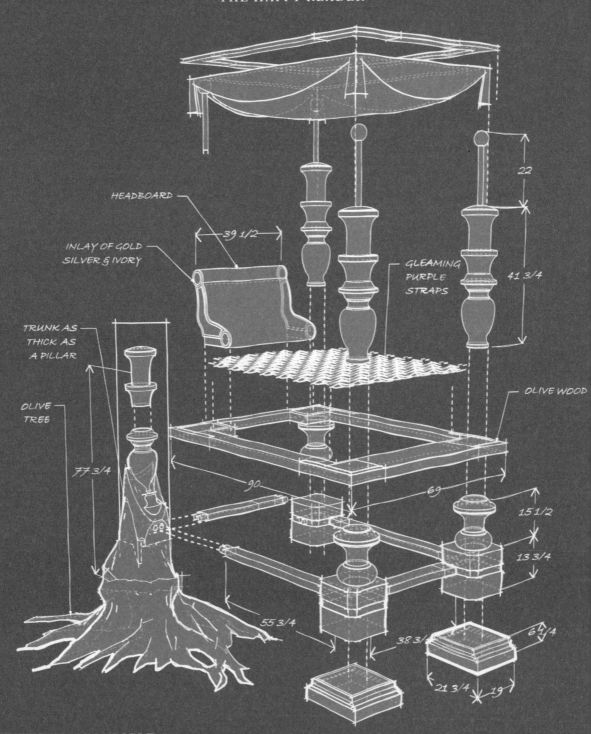

HEADBOARD

INLAY OF GOLD
SILVER & IVORY

TRUNK AS
THICK AS
A PILLAR

OLIVE
TREE

GLEAMING
PURPLE
STRAPS

OLIVE WOOD

39 1/2

22

41 3/4

77 3/4

90

69

15 1/2

13 3/4

55 3/4

38 3/4

6 1/4

21 3/4    19

## DO IT YOURSELF

'Inside the court there was a long-leaved olive-tree, which had grown to full height with a trunk as thick as a pillar… I lopped all the branches off the olive, trimmed the trunk from the root up, rounded it smoothly and carefully with my adze and trued it to the line, to be my bedpost. I drilled holes in it, and using it as the first bedpost I constructed the rest of the bed. Then I finished it off with an inlay of gold, silver and ivory, and fixed a set of gleaming purple straps across the frame.' Odysseus's bed-making technique, transposed into a blueprint by designer-artist TODD VAN HULZEN.

'The Coen brothers did this bit well in *O Brother, Where Art Thou?*' noted Lias.

'Oh yeah. With John Goodman as the Cyclops.'

Now dozing Odysseus is roused by the girls' frolicking.

'How old are we saying Odysseus is?' Lias asked. 'About forty?'

'Mhmm, that's what I was thinking.'

Nausicaa takes Odysseus down to the water with her girls for a good bathing and oiling, after which he is a new man, a real sight for these frisky young babes. Any moment now it could all go Henry Miller, but instead Odysseus shows himself to be, 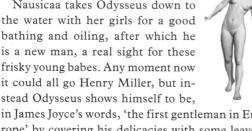 in James Joyce's words, 'the first gentleman in Europe' by covering his delicacies with some leaves to avoid offending the girls' modesty. It's the desire of every forty-year-old man to be bathed and oiled by considerate young beauties: he hopes to impress such nubiles with his worldly air of having seen a few things and sailed the open seas, fought alongside heroes and feasted with legends. Or perhaps I should speak only for myself and admit I'd love to be where Odysseus is now, led to the palace by Nausicaa and her smiling girlfriends, there to meet her parents, King Alcinous and Queen Arete.

★ ★ ★

We read a chapter sitting on the grass in the evening sun at Volkspark Friedrichshain. King Alcinous lays on a big party for homesick Odysseus. To get things going, he calls out the bard Demodocus, 'prized by all the people'. Demodocus is Homer's advertisement for himself, his sly way of  insisting on the importance of the bard's gift while reminding us that in the halls of the flashiest kings, the song-and-dance man is always well looked after. The art of spinning yarns and living to tell the tale is as old as the Olympian hills, but so too is the desire to make it at least a bit about yourself. The knack has ever been to realise you're already living inside a book, then write it down. This is what Homer is getting at when he has Alcinous comfort an Odysseus bummed out by the horrors of war by telling him:

*That is the gods' work, spinning threads of death*
*through the lives of mortal men,*
*and all to make a song for those to come...*

Nicely baked as the sun set on a thirty-seven-degree scorcher, it struck me with stoner-visionary force that *we* were 'those to come' — at once listening to this ancient song and living out the rhythms and melodies to the song of the future. It barely mattered whether your life rang out tragic or comic — in a war zone or in peacetime, in glory or dishonour — so long as the story was a good one. In fact, if unspeakable calamities did not beset the course of your life, arguably something was missing — there was no odyssey without terror and monsters. To listen to the great song was to *participate* in it — and a deeper participation still was this remix and retelling that my friend and I were engaged in, living the book over a few stoned weeks in the late Berlin summer to produce this wayward commentary, which in turn snapshots a heightened and delirious moment when everything became mythic, became Homeric, became *the song*.

For all our euphoria, Lias and I were beginning to feel irked by Daddy O's moaning: 'What pains — the gods have given me my share.' It's a bit emo, a bit softboy, not in keeping with the manly warrior ethos that elsewhere holds sway in Homer, who generally provokes delighted alertness to life's wine-dark sensual richness, its narrative flair. Speaking of wine, there are rivers of it in *The Odyssey*, always labelled with a loving adjective or two:

 'mellow wine'; 'heady wine'; 'a big full-bodied wine'; 'heart-warming wine'; 'glowing wine'; 'seasoned wine'; 'the deep-red mellow vintage'; 'strong neat wine', 'ruddy, irresistible wine'; 'powerful wine'; 'a fine libation', 'honeyed wine'; and scene after scene soaked in 'much wine to swill'.

On Saturday afternoon, following a night in the subterranean nightclub Tresor, we sat on the balcony with a pot of tea and read two more chapters. After a hairy detour in the land of the Cyclops, Odysseus and crew finally get in sight of land — Ithaca itself! — only to blow it at the last minute by opening the sack of winds they'd been gifted by some  sorcerer or other. When they wash up at the beautiful goddess Circe's palace on her island of Aeaea, 'the nymph with lovely braids' drugs them. They're always getting drugged — I wouldn't be surprised if they were letting it happen, feigning not to notice all these sultry females slip a little something into their drinks. (Lias: 'It sounds like being on the road with my band.') There's a bit of typical nymph fuckery when Circe transforms Big O's men into pigs, then seduces the hero in another hot scene. Odysseus has been sexually harassed at every stage of his journey, but that's the least of his worries now because this chapter ends on a real cliffhanger, as Circe informs the anguished crew that they must descend into the Kingdom of the Dead...

That night, at the Kitkat Club, we lay back in the cushions around the swimming pool and took

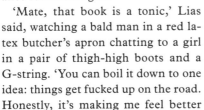

in the banquet of beauty and flamboyance surrounding us.

'Mate, that book is a tonic,' Lias said, watching a bald man in a red latex butcher's apron chatting to a girl in a pair of thigh-high boots and a G-string. 'You can boil it down to one idea: things get fucked up on the road.

Honestly, it's making me feel better about the catastrophes I've lived through. You get so caught up in that shit while it's happening, but then you read this and you see it's an old, old story. Things just get fucked up.'

Right next to us, a perfectly toned, bronzed warrior with a dark beard and flowing hair began to expertly finger two nubile girls reclining beneath him. We turned to gawp, unconcerned about coming over voyeuristic at what was, after all, a public sexual display.

'He's one of Odysseus' shipmates,' Lias said into my ear, a little too loudly. 'Look at that face, that focus. He's a man of purpose, a man of action. Him and his nymphs. He'll do whatever it takes to get home to Ithaca. He'll get out and push if he has to. Look at him. Knuckle deep in Dawn with her rose-red fingers, and her no less fetching sister. Don't you think the blonde one looks like Roisin? Go on, lad! *Ithaca!*'

★ ★ ★

We ran out of brownies that weekend, so we waded through the next couple of chapters amid an unsoftened hangover. Following some misadventures in the Kingdom of the Dead and the island of the sun-god Hyperion, Odysseus is ferried across the seas by the Phaeacians in a magical ship. Finally! This is it, his *nostos*, his homecoming, in a chapter with the stirring title 'Ithaca at Last'. We can't help but notice that this homecoming takes place only halfway through the book, meaning that the latter half of the epic about a journey home takes

place *at* home. How will Homer keep us *riveted*? What's even going on in the writers' room? Speaking of rooms, there was an elephant in this one.

'He's been away twenty years,' said Lias. 'What if he's stopped fancying his wife?'

'It's true she's no longer in her prime', I replied. 'But then, neither is he. Maybe Penelope gives him a sense of security, confidence...'

'But he's already encountered everything there was to be insecure *about*, and he's survived. I'm not saying Penelope isn't seriously desirable. But attachments fade, the heart moves on. Meanwhile, all these nymphs and sex goddesses are flinging themselves at the man and we're meant to believe he'd give it all up to get back to his wife of two decades hence? It's starting to look like a plot hole.'

The goddess Athena coats Ithaca in mist and disguises Odysseus as an old beggar. Questioned by an islander as to his identity, he spins an origin yarn in which he includes himself — the real Odysseus — as a peripheral character, described in the third person: 'That's when I first got wind of *him* — Odysseus.' The fake autobiographical tale is not *completely* invented, but reads rather like a remixed dream of Odysseus' own life, with settings and details changed but the basic experiential truth of his journeys and great trials intact — which shows that when it comes to self-reflexive postmodernist meta-trickery, nobody beats the ancients. There's talk of various gods and noteworthy mortals, including one 'Clitus' — presumably this is the god of clitorises, to whose cult the *CLIT* graffiti all over Ber-

lin pays homage. Prompted to tell his own life story, a swineherd named Eumaeus urges

his audience to settle in for a good yarn in a passage that may as well be Homer inviting me and Lias and all his readers down the rolling centuries:

*listen in quiet, then, and take your ease, sit back*
*and drink your wine. The nights are endless now.*
*We've plenty of time to sleep or savor a long tale.*

★ ★ ★

At this point in our journey, I found myself alone. After accompanying me for two-thirds of my odyssey, Lias left Berlin on a London-bound train, and the following day Roisin flew home ahead of me to Dublin. That evening I read aloud to myself the

*Greek gods at a gathering, as depicted by British artist Roger Payne*

chapter in which Odysseus-in-disguise enters his palace for the first time in two decades, enduring blows and insults as he does so. It was good stuff but I missed reading with Lias — and he and Roisin weren't the only companions who'd deserted me. In my second-hand copy of *The Odyssey* a previous owner had underlined passages in blue pen, adding emphatic stars and simple marginal notes ('Turns men into pigs', 'Fame', 'Sending mother away'). While reading with Lias I'd warmed to the company of this fellow-traveller, who I imagined as the female third in our readerly threesome. I'd enjoyed seeing which points along the route she'd considered noteworthy, relating to her like a friend you make on some backpacker's trail who keeps popping up further along the way. My red-pen markings complimented hers in a pleasing bi-coloured duet. But when Lias left, so did she. Her underlinings ceased at the very chapter from which I voyaged on alone — our *ménage à trois* was over.

By Book 20 Odysseus is still mooching about on Ithaca, building up for his big vengeance. We're getting a little impatient, blasphemously wondering — as Roddy Doyle quipped about Joyce's *Ulysses* — if Homer could have done with an editor. We know that two chapters down the line we'll come to the climactic 'Slaughter in the Hall' and every nerve craves that catharsis. In Book 21, 'Odysseus Strings His Bow', Homer walks his narrative right to the brink of the promised bloodbath...

An opportune moment to pause and wonder again about those too-hopeful suitors. Rather than try to understand their motives within a framework of psychological realism (which wouldn't be around for centuries yet), we ought instead to take the suitors as a swarming symbol of male sexual insecurity. The cover blurb of my copy of the epic partly reads, '*The Odyssey* is literature's grandest evocation of everyman's journey through life', and in those horny suitors we discern everyman's primal fear and challenge. The predicament is universal: a man loves a pretty woman, and the price he pays for this love is the tormenting certainty that at all times a horde of other men are hovering just out of view, ready to pounce the moment he falters. They're sliding into her DMs, crowding her memories, quickening her daydreams — and our embattled everyman must bat them off or else lose his queen.

Odysseus, though, has the air of a man who can sexually hold his own.

It's true he's getting on a bit, past the priapic bloom of youth, and yet Penelope wants one dick and one dick only — his — and he knows it. How can this be? The answer is in the adjective that attaches recurrently to his name in this chapter, often rasped from the mouths of rivals such as crestfallen fuck-boy Eurymachus:

*What breaks my heart is the fact we fall so short*
*of great Odysseus' strength we cannot string his bow.*
*A disgrace to ring in the ears of men to come.*

Greatness. That's what keeps Big O desirable as the flesh slackens and the quick brilliance of youth recedes. And here we find another tentative moral in this largely amoral story: to stay attractive to women or to hold on to the one he has, *a man must become great*. The  greatness he achieves might be sporting or artistic, martial or political, or it might be the quieter greatness of being a good father and protector. But if a man doesn't rise to the odyssean challenge of life *by becoming great*, he's screwed.

Hovering at the threshold, I texted Lias in Brixton: 'Fancy tuning in for "Slaughter in the Hall"? The climax we've been waiting for. Feels wrong to read it on my own.'

'Wish I could but we've been offered last-minute festival gigs in France at the weekend. Manna from heaven. Rehearsing now.'

I'd have to go it alone. After midnight, as a much-needed rainstorm cooled Berlin, I got to it — and was plunged straight into the carnage. Bellowing about 'black doom', Odysseus raises his bow and commences the slaughter in a scene that recalls the jihadist massacres and school shootings that terrorise today's West: the exits sealed, the victims trapped like chickens on the killing floor, the panic and stampede. One poor sap thinks he can save himself by getting on his knees to beg for mercy — Odysseus lops his head off. A tramp is dragged outside to have his cock ripped off and fed to the dogs. Perhaps the nastiest coda comes when  the female staff are summoned to clean up after the orgy of killing. They get to work sopping up blood, clearing away the bodies — but this is a ruse allowing Big O to enact a cruel patriarchal vengeance. Even though back in Book 9 Odysseus had bragged about pirate raids in which he'd made off with much 'wives and plunder', he's disgusted by these women — 'You sluts

— the suitors' whores!' — and orders his son to brutally execute them.

★ ★ ★

It was all over bar the coda. I read the final chapter, 'Peace', while naked on a deckchair on my balcony in the late-August sun, the day after a last raid on the techno dungeons. Down  in the netherworld the slaughtered suitors are keen to tell their side of the story — an aggrieved account which presages our stormy contemporary debates about power discourse, systemic inequality and all the rest of it. Aware that posterity is going to shit on them, the suitors hash out their version of events in the hope of gaining a cult following who will insist down the centuries that Odysseus was a straight white dick and they were the true victims. They even resort to smearing Penelope with some Depp v. Heard-style vitriol:

*…the song men sing of her will ring with loathing.*
*She brands with foul name the breed of womankind,*
*even the honest ones to come!*

Back on earth, the fathers of the slain suitors are so enraged that a whole new war seems imminent, which would neatly tee up another lucrative sequel (*Iliad 2: Troy Harder*) and set the stage for what will doubtless become known as the 'Homer universe' — but then Athena steps in, offers a prayer to Papa Zeus, and orders them all to 'make peace at once!'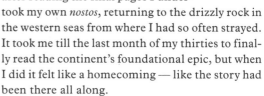

And so *The Odyssey* ends — but of course it never really ends. A few days after reading the final pages I undertook my own *nostos*, returning to the drizzly rock in the western seas from where I had so often strayed. It took me till the last month of my thirties to finally read the continent's foundational epic, but when I did it felt like a homecoming — like the story had been there all along.

ROB DOYLE is the Dublin-born author of four internationally acclaimed books: *Autobibliography*, *Threshold*, *This Is the Ritual* and *Here Are the Young Men*, which has been adapted for film. His writing has appeared in the *New York Times*, *Observer*, *Dublin Review* and many other publications.

# Five Crossword Clues To Which The Answer Is 'The Odyssey'

1. Vainglorious description of minor adminis-
   trative ordeal
2. 24-episode arc where Homer sells a minivan?
3. Triumph of good over evil: bad homonym
4. Abnormal affirmation sent back to middle
   Huxtable child
5. Surrounded by epicene army, scoop vichy-
   ssoise by close of business

Their setter, DANIEL LEVIN BECKER,
is an American writer and translator and a
member of the French literary group Oulipo.

# THE PENGUIN CLASSICS

A LIBRARY OF NEW TRANSLATIONS

edited by E. V. Rieu

1. HOMER : The Odyssey         *E. V. Rieu*

*

IN PREPARATION

*From the Greek*

HOMER : The Iliad         *E. V. Rieu*
SOPHOCLES : The Theban Plays    *E. F. Watling*
XENOPHON : The Persian Expedition   *Rex Warner*
THEOCRITUS : The Idyls         *Adeline Cook*

*From the Latin*

TACITUS : On Germany and Britain   *H. Mattingly*

*From the Italian*

DANTE : The Divine Comedy    *Dorothy L. Sayers*

*From the French*

VOLTAIRE : Candide         *John Butt*
MAUPASSANT : The Olive Grove
     and Other Stories      *H. N. P. Sloman*

*From the Russian*

TURGENIEV : On the Eve      *G. C. Gardiner*
GORKI : Childhood        *Elizabeth Gow*

*From the Norwegian*

IBSEN : Pillars of Society, The Wild
     Duck, Hedda Gabler     *Una Ellis-Fermor*

*

PENGUIN BOOKS LIMITED
LONDON AND NEW YORK

'A classic is a book that has never finished saying what it has to say,' writes Italo Calvino. Every ending is also a beginning. The back cover of the 1946 edition of *The Odyssey* marked the launch of the list known as the Penguin Classics. Of course, Penguin Classics would go on to become one of the world's most famous publishing imprints and then, for this most recent decade, publisher of a new kind of literary magazine in the form of *The Happy Reader*. Thank you for reading.